New
Directions in
Japanese
Architecture

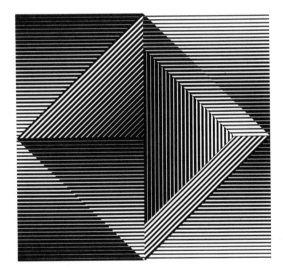

ROBIN BOYD

NEW DIRECTIONS

IN

JAPANESE

ARCHITECTURE

STUDIO VISTA   LONDON

First published 1968 in London by

Studio Vista Limited, Blue Star House, Highgate Hill,

London N 19

SBN 289 79564 x

and in New York by

George Braziller, Inc. One Park Avenue, New York, N.Y. 10016

Library of Congress Catalog Card Number 68-29665

Designed by Jennie Bush

Printed in U.S.A.

First Printing

CONTENTS

THE INESCAPABLE
TRADITION

THE world knows Japanese architecture best by two faces. One is all delicacy and lightness, slippered feet on *tatami*, naked timber ceilings, and silently sliding paper *shoji* screens. It may be called Tourist Traditional because it is not the only relic of the tradition, but just the most obvious one. The other face is full of force and conviction, hefty concrete and tensioned steel. It may be called Architects' Modern, because it is not the only manifestation of new architecture, but just the most professional one. It is the proud new style of Japan. No country has developed out of the international elements of modern architecture a more distinctive one more quickly. It is the subject of this essay.

This proud new style of Japan and her best-known formal tradition may seem, at first sight, to be at opposite poles of art and civilization. The traditional was simple, sometimes to a degree of austerity that makes the severest of all Western styles—the Greek—seem vulgar. The modern is intricate, complex and attracted to richness despite its commitment to stripped concrete.

The traditional was mystical and symbolic: a flat bowl of water or a chirping cricket in a cage suggesting coolness in a suffocating paper-thin summer house. The modern stands for tough realism and air conditioning.

The traditional was usually slender and minimal; light, subtle and feminine. The modern is usually heavy, sometimes coarse, generally aggressively masculine.

The traditional was poetic, intuitive, visual. The modern is logical and intellectual: an ideal architecture with quite enough strength to be anti-aesthetic when it wants to be, which is the most unforgivable affront to the traditional sensibilities.

The traditional was socially classless and cumulative. The modern is esoteric. That is to say, the Architects' Modern which the world recognizes as distinctively Japanese is by no means an expression of the people. It shares with much of modern Western architecture the danger of being too exclusive, an art for the little world of architects and architecture fanciers.

Yet all these contrasts between the traditional and the modern do not result from an avant-garde movement oblivious to the past, as a Western one may be. On the contrary, almost every step the modern Japanese takes shows his awareness of tradition and his deliberate attempt to rid himself of shallow imitation of it. Thus the extreme contrasts. The young modern Japanese does not reject the traditions which lately have been so warmly admired by the West. He accepts the beauty of the Ise Shrines and the Katsura Palace without losing his breath and stores them in his mind next to the Parthenon and medieval cathedrals. Any conflicts of design philosophy within him are not concerned with reconciling East and West. All that is at least a generation behind now. Nevertheless, the Japanese visual traditions are so intense that even expatriate Japanese artists are never quite rid of them and those at home are continuously under their influence, whether they want to be or not. Even if the modern architects can escape the historical trimmings and associations, the introversion and the withdrawal, their historical background is still alive with unforgettable evocative forms and images.

There are, for instance, the sublime curves: geometrically free but aesthetically pure. The very essence of traditional Japanese design is conveyed to Western eyes by a vigorous, often unexpected curve climaxing a precise formation of straight lines: the curve of the cope or beam over the upright gateposts of a Shinto Shrine, the silhouette of roof ridges bent as if sagging under the weight of centuries with their ends tilting up toward the mountains, the arch of a wooden bridge made of short straight timbers, the long straight tapered handle of a hand implement expanding into functional curves at its business end, the paper arcs of the fan and the parasol on their thin radial spars, the sudden gratuitous curves in a straight raking of gravel.

The traditional embraces numerous other formal design elements that are equally characteristic and evocative of Japan, forms that are at their root symbols of the desire for an elemental harmony between the artificial thing and nature, forms suggestive of metaphysical overtones, as in the arrangement of fifteen rocks in the garden at the Ryoanji Temple at Kyoto, placed so that no more than fourteen can be seen at any time. Other related formal devices include the castoff stone which artfully breaks a line of stepping stones, the beam that passes through and projects beyond its supporting post, and deliberate asymmetry where least expected. Then within each group of forms there are the characteristic techniques and materials: the thin precise sticks of wood in rhythmic grids and grilles, the timber panels, thatch, paper, pebbles—all unsullied by paint or varnish and soft with the feel and smell of the forest.

The shapes, techniques and textures of traditional Japan made up a vocabulary rather than a discipline for the designer. Most of them are classifiable as to historic, social, religious or geographical origins. They also may be categorized as to character—as between, for instance, the formal, aristocratic, more feminine Yayoi and the vital, more masculine and vulgar Jomon culture.

The Japanese vocabulary recognizes fine distinctions between various aesthetic qualities which the English language can hardly explain in a paragraph, let alone a word. Yet no amount of analysis and categorizing can loosen the ties that bind all the elements of historical Japanese design into a visual identity which is at least as different from its historical antecedents—the Chinese and Korean—as Roman was from Greek.

The young Japanese architect of this last third of the twentieth century has grown up with tradition close around him. No doubt his family crest is of a characteristic traditional shape. But he feels heir to the whole world's ancient culture as well as to its newest technologies. Usually he is as rebellious by nature as all creative artists must be, and he feels obliged to try to reject tradition as sentimental and restricting. Nevertheless, he is drawn back to the forms of Japan again and again, as many of the illustrations herein testify. And this is inevitable, for the twentieth-century architecture which a generation ago the West gave to Japan, mainly by way of Le Corbusier, was thick with theories and ethics into which much of the Japanese tradition fitted as if it had always belonged. In fact, Western civilization found it necessary to have an intellectual revolution some three thousand years after it began creating architecture, in order to arrive at roughly the same elemental approach to building that Japan had as a matter of course from the beginning.

Many qualities in the Japanese tradition match emotionally the most advanced mood of international architecture. These include the love of naked materials, the delight in open space at the expense of partitions and furnishing impedimenta, the pleasure of demonstrating the structural means of support, and the satisfaction in the use of a module. Indeed, the module of the hand-prefabricated, one by two meters *tatami* floor mat, whose dimensions and layouts dictated room sizes, makes the most remarkable philosophical link between Japanese traditional and the international modern, which has always enjoyed conforming to industrial standards. The Japanese traditional even had a respect for function as the departure point of design that is closer to the international modern mood than anything in official historical Western architecture.

Thus, if a rebellious young Japanese architect of this moment wants to remake the world in the image of great and true architecture, he is bound not to reject his heritage—the tradition—but to move toward its heart. His real problem is to find its heart. As it has already been suggested, the search for a true architecture does not illuminate all building in modern Japan. Such stirring architectural sights as are recorded in this book do not exactly crowd in on the visitor to Japan. He has to search for them. He probably first sees Japan from the freeway or the monorail which runs eight miles or so from Tokyo's international airport to terminal points close to the city center. All this apparatus of arrival is impeccably done, as smooth, trim and beautifully mannered as the white-gloved attendants, and it represents the principal style of modern Japan, which is routine commercial-industrial Functionalism.

Parts of the elevated freeway and the massive twin concrete monorails on their T supports interweave en route, flying over the shallows of Tokyo Bay, above canals lined with barges and little old wooden houses with vine-covered verandas, above steelyards, junk heaps, and gray sheds and the rest of the mess that is the world's biggest city.

The vulgarity which the young Japanese architect has to confront is rather different from the extroverted Western kind. Some appalling plastic trinkets give evidence of a soft core of visual delinquency growing behind private *shoji*, but in the public street there is little that is comparable to the Western concept of bad taste. The taste and color of most buildings is simply gray. There is a preoccupied, monochromatic untidiness in place of the varicolored visual competition of the West. Behind the night lights and the pink and green commercial decorations, there are acres of fairly shabby gray concrete and gray glass. The roofs are a darker gray. The tangle of telephone and power wires makes a gray net above charcoal roads. The very air is often a smoggy gray. Most of the buildings seem just to have happened, exhibiting no taste at all. But against this vast negative background, ranging from the mechanical to the careless, stylists and decorators have been adding—during two decades or so—the trimmings which presumably delight the tourists while bemusing the natives. These are the caricatures of the tradition, details dragged screaming from the past to be stuck on to modern concrete: wood grilles, picket screens, lanterns, drooping beams over doorways. A spectacular example is the Hotel Empire in the Yokohama "Dreamland," a square needle skyscraper transformed by drooping eaves at every floor to look something like a pagoda of the Momoyama Period, but one twenty-two stories high. Such things repel the more sensitive Japanese, while they muddy the tradition and make the finding of its real meaning a difficult, personal search for many architects today.

In their revolt against such shameless and effete visual trickiness, most architects who began practice after World War II understandably sought strength and realism. It is not surprising that they should have found their closest soulmate among all the modern masters of the West to be another who had revolted against an oversophisticated, ingrown culture: Le Corbusier of Paris. In modern Japan one can find small traces of influence of nearly all the other Western leaders: Saarinen geometry, Wrightian horizontality, Yamasaki arcades, Rudolph ribbed concrete, Kahn pylons; but the overriding influence is the one which Kunio Mayekawa and Junzo Sakakura, two of the fathers of Japanese Modern, brought back with them from the studios of Le Corbusier. Nothing else had quite the grasp of reality, the gusto and the guts that the Japanese were looking for. Thus the postwar generation of Japanese architects used Le Corbusier as a stepping stone out of the past to avoid parodies of the past. They took as their model the most adaptable Corbu genre, the Corbu of Marseilles and Chandigarh, which was marked by stripped concrete of prodigious dimensions and a sort of hierarchy of contrasted forms. Le Corbusier would adopt a comparatively simple basic form and set it up in undisputed domination; but he would also introduce numerous subforms and sub-subforms, most of which suggested with reasonable conviction that they were answering specific functional demands. In the Japanese version the basic form was often more adventurous, sometimes alarmingly so, while the subforms were often more inscrutable and the concrete even more gargantuan.

That was for a few years the ruling postwar style of Japan, but in a remarkably short time—no more than a decade—the balance became much steadier on the stepping stone and Japan was ready for an independent step forward. That step was duly taken, but only very recently. Whether or not Japan is committed to the new direction is still not clear, although one may make guesses from the sum of the illustrations in these pages. At the worst, the new Japanese architects may make some sensational splashes in the private pool of the world architectural establishment. Yet they may do much more. They may succeed in doing what their leaders hope to do: to restore a genuine elemental approach to popular building, involving the ordinary Japanese man and woman as design used to do in the tradition, but in the techniques of the new technology.

THE SPACE PSYCHOSIS

ONLY one of the major social factors influencing the growth of creative buildings and cities in Japan is quite different from anything in Western architecture. The other factors are familiar, although the problems are often more intense. Over-all hangs the massive challenge of urban and regional planning. In Japan these operations are dominated by problems of inadequate space. It used to be said that eighty percent of the country was uninhabitable, consisting only of mountains, beautiful from afar, but ragged and uninviting for living. These, however, may yet have to be made habitable, and already some are being sliced into, or lopped or leveled, for various installations, because on the remaining twenty percent of flat land the population of Japan is crowded at an average of 3,500 per square mile. On the whole, the population density of Japan is ten times that of the United States. There is a pervading feeling of constriction, and smallness of scale. Even the open countryside looks as if it has just been hand-finished by a fastidious modelmaker. In the cities, and especially in Tokyo, the pressure of the twentieth century on an ancient web of spidery streets and flimsy, inflammable houses has seemed to be at tearing point continuously for about two decades. The proportion of the total urban area devoted to streets is usually no more than one third of the Western average, and then the streets often seem hardly wider than a car. Yet the modern Japanese has to be just as mobile as his contemporaries elsewhere, is becoming just about as car-conscious, and is fonder than most people of traveling in his own country for pleasure.

The problems inside Tokyo were bad enough in 1960 when Kenzo Tange felt obliged by his position of eminence in Japanese architecture to volunteer a solution. He published A Plan for Tokyo which showed how order could be brought to the megalopolis in four five-year stages. His idea was to draw out the present single central hub into a linear spine extending into Tokyo Bay. However, the four stages were not especially easy ones and although photographs of Tange's remarkable model have become famous and influential around the world there was never any real hope at home of the plan being implemented. The enormous cost of putting any bold planning scheme into practice has so far been rather more intimidating than the results of congestion. The celebrated pressure-packing of travelers on suburban trains will have to get worse, the virtual curfew that operates downtown to allow waiters and workers time to get home will have to creep earlier into the evening, the traffic will have to tangle more madly before drastic action becomes absolutely essential. In the meantime the dangerous condition is relieved with cautious doses of palliative. The Government's Greater Capital Sphere Law designates an area of 200 kilometers in diameter as the Greater Metropolitan Area for Tokyo and seeks to put some order into development in this zone. Nevertheless, in a country as tightly packed as Japan the planning problems of the capital cannot be isolated by a zoning ordinance. Tokyo grows by a million people every three years, but its citizens are not alarmed by this; they are proud to be part of the world's largest city. It runs into Yokohama without a pause for breath and it is now tied to the twelve million people of the great Kobe-Osaka industrial complex by the Tokaido line high-speed railway. Planners like Professor Eika Takayama of Tokyo University call fruitlessly for developmental planning on a national scale.

Throughout the reconstruction since World War II the Government's policy within local zones has been one of moderate encouragement and partial subsidy of the most vital improvements, such as untangling the street web to provide city blocks big enough to carry sizable modern buildings, and changing over to fire-resistant construction. As a result of this encouragement, the use of concrete and masonry has grown at the expense of wood from ten percent of all construction at the beginning of postwar reconstruction to sixty percent at present. The Government also empowers city authorities to requisition land for rebuilding in certain prescribed areas, and gives some financial assistance to slum clearance and to the building of housing, which now proceeds at the rate of about one million units a year.

Even with the subsidies, and despite the outward appearance of a high living standard, the pressure on space seeps indoors. With the exception of a few rich custom-built houses, mostly designed by architects, the size of all new dwellings is diminutive. The living space in apartments built under the Government housing plan is small compared with both traditional Japanese and modern Western standards. It is often, in fact, much less than half the size of an equivalent Western apartment. Two small rooms usually serve a family. Smaller apartments being built in 1968 have bathroom facilities shared between two family units. Even the early elevated freeways have four lanes so narrow that speed is limited.

The reason for the persistence of a scale which is perceptibly smaller than the world norm is partly economic and partly conditioned by a consciousness that the Japanese are people of shorter stature (though they are catching up now); but it is also partly a folk habit. Certainly it was not in the classic tradition. The spaces in the great shrines and palaces were often vast and open. The interior of the Izumo Shrine was more than 100 meters high; the ancient city of Nara was planned on a vast scale, under Chinese influence. Yet an ingredient of the wistful beauty of the Japanese vernacular tradition was its leaning toward a minimum scale. And this is one of the qualities which has helped to shape the new architecture of Japan—simply because the new architects react against it. They will have none of it. They are engrossed with questions of space and scale, and they tend invariably to the maximum scale possible under any given set of circumstances. "I want to create spaces on a scale beyond the human and then return those spaces to human beings," writes Professor Kazuo Shinohara,[1] and he is not speaking of public buildings but of the small houses which he builds.

Despite all economies, the task of reconstructing Japanese cities is colossal, and the Japanese people are conspicuously not civic-minded. The contrast between dirt and dilapidation in public places and impeccable cleanliness indoors is one of the most remarkable characteristics of modern Japanese life. Most of the expenditure of public money on the improvements that have been made thus far would not have been politically or socially acceptable but for the introduction of an artificial stimulus.

The stimulus in the case of Tokyo was the 1964 Olympic Games. Tokyo allowed itself five years to prepare for them, but the characteristic indifference of the Japanese to their public environment operated till the date of the Games came perilously close. Then, suddenly, a frenzy of construction carried to completion, just in time, a spectacular network of railways—on, above and below ground—and freeways, parks, recreation complexes, and hotels. The total investment amounted to about $2.5 billion, not including expenses directly associated with the Games. The stimulus in the case of Osaka is Expo 70—the World Exposition of 1970—and at the time of writing it promises to do for that city, perhaps at a slightly reduced scale, what the Olympic Games did for Tokyo.

Architects and planners throughout Japan, however, will tell you that something much bolder is required. It might have been expected that the Japanese, as late starters in modern architecture, would be content for a while to conduct the revolution by guerilla tactics: one brave new building at a time. On the contrary, they have been even more aware than most others that the promise of twentieth-century architecture is still obscured by ignorance, pettiness and economic restrictions. They realize more than most of their busy contemporaries elsewhere how thankless and futile it is to sweat over the perfection of one pure gem of a building when it will be set in a slum of wire and signs and commercial expediency. Like all modern architects they carry on their consciences the burden of the modern mess, and so they are in the thick of the dramatic international avant-garde pursuit of the next era, when technology swings at last to building: the Age of the Megastructure.

For half a century or more architects in many places have been predicting the next necessary phase of design: the breakout from the limitations of precious one-of-a-kind buildings. They see the forces of progress demanding and securing much greater scope for design activity: cities, regions, ultimately the whole world ordered and illuminated by the ideals of design, about which there is no real argument. The younger architects of Japan are perhaps less disillusioned and cynical than those of the West and have faith in the feasibility of such a vision within measurable time.

The Japanese architects' declaration of independence was the World Design Conference in Tokyo in 1960, just as soon as they began to feel secure in the new genre. It was a deliberate bid to pull Japan into the middle of world architecture, and it succeeded to a great extent in focusing the new movement. At the sharpest point there formed an association calling itself the Metabolism Group. Metabolism was dedicated to a new world pervaded by creative, endlessly expanding architecture. It was led by Kiyonori Kikutake, then aged thirty-two, with Noriaki Kurokawa and the critic Noboru Kawazoe. Other architects including Asada, Oe and Maki, as well as some planners, painters and allied designers, followed along in spirit. They set themselves against the closed forms and mean scale of conventional modern building. They were closely related by their fantastic visions to another, slightly later association of young enthusiasts in another crowded island: the British Archigram Group, which now claims some Japanese adherents, and has collaborated with the Metabolists. The basis of both movements is impatience with the way the world has been picking at the problem of the modern city and playing around the edge of constructional technology. Both tackle the problem of obsolescence by proposing structures so free that they can adapt to any advances in technology. Both have no patience with the realities of municipal politics and private ownership. Both create images of megastructures, buildings big enough to carry a city's population, but so basic and adaptable that they may be no more than skeletons or masts to carry mechanical services. Both are concerned with a noticeable inconsistency in current technological development: the disproportionate rate of progress between the mass-manufactured items of equipment and the individually constructed shells that house them.

By the end of this century radical changes are likely to occur in the electronic, electrical and mechanical accessories inside our shelters, in lighting, air conditioning, audio and visual intercommunication, water conservation, vertical and horizontal transport, and other comforts not yet invented. Buildings now being constructed solidly enough to last two centuries or so will inevitably be operationally obsolete before this century ends. Must they then be painfully torn down while still so young? What waste and inefficiency (not to mention the end of architecture as a persistent record of culture)! Thus, to be realistic, buildings should either accept that they are dispensable, in which case they should be made much more readily destructible, perhaps with exposed bolted joints, or they should recognize that they have a dual nature. They should have spaces made for people, whose basic spatial requirements have not changed much over the centuries, and parts made for the equipment which serves and refines those spaces, and is even now only in its infancy. Thus the spaces may be permanent (permitting architecture to continue its historic monumental role) while the servicing parts should be brought out of their hiding places in the walls and ceilings to be as removable and renewable as a refrigerator in a kitchen. This virtually commits the servicing parts to different materials and forms divorced from the main building, and to a prominence they never enjoyed in the past. The Metabolists recognize Louis Kahn's Richards Laboratories at the University of Pennsylvania, with its clearly separated service pylons, as a trail-blazer in the realization of this analytical concept.

In the restless, fervent dream images of the Metabolists (or the Archigrams) the house is usually considered to be a unit too small for anyone to bother analyzing into separate living spaces and servant parts; the whole house unit is a dispensable piece of mass-produced equipment like a car, to be traded-in and renewed when outgrown. Alternatively, and more sentimentally, sometimes the house unit is considered a relic of folklore, something almost unworthy of an architect's attention and which might safely be left to the whims of the occupants. In either case the householder eventually seeks a megastructure in which to insert his living unit. And when he is lucky enough to catch one stationary—for some walk or float—he slips his house in or clips it on, plugging in for the electrical and electronic comforts.

That, however, is only the primitive start of Metabolist thinking. From there it wades gradually deeper and deeper into metaphysics. The ferment of Japanese architectural philosophy is well-illustrated by its obscure and extravagant language. The concepts tumble over each other in an undergraduate kind of enthusiasm and confusion. To Metabolism they add a string of architectural allegories. Topological space, entropy, fusion, polymerization, fibrous form and porous spaces are among their conversational terms that seek to equate architecture to organic or chemical order.

Young Japanese architects tirelessly produce drawings and models of their own visionary cities growing along such lines, and many of these are involved also with the special Japanese need to increase the space available for living. In two of the first of the long sequence of visions, Kiyonori Kikutake achieved extra space in the two most obvious and convenient ways. In Marine City he built on and under the water (*Fig. 1*). In Tower City he skyscraped (*Fig. 2*). These designs were published as Metabolism Group projects, though

1. *Kiyonori Kikutake: Marine City, drawing, 1958.*

2. *Kiyonori Kikutake: Tower City, section, 1959.*

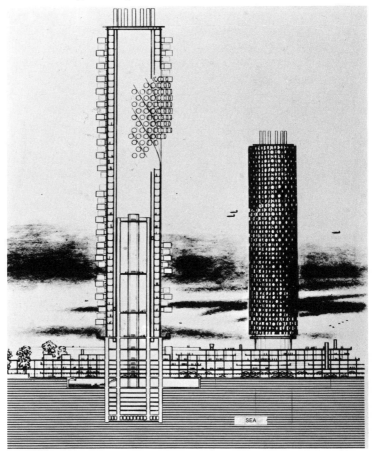

in fact they were developed earlier, independently, by Kikutake, and prompted the formation of the group.

In a slightly later scheme—Helix City by Noriaki Kurokawa—more space was created by building artificial "land" in the form of giant multilevel towers twisted to throw their platforms open to the sun and air (*Fig 3*). The artificial land idea was seen first in a comparatively modest hypothetical project on which Kenzo Tange directed his students when he was a Visiting Professor at the Massachusetts Institute of Technology in 1959–60. In his Plan for Tokyo he developed the idea again, suggesting giant tentlike structures with draped sides hanging over the water of Tokyo Bay.

A competition run by the magazine *Shinkenchiku* in 1966 for

3. *Noriaki Kurokawa: Helix City, drawing, 1962.*

4. *Akira Shibuya: Prize-winning project, model, 1966.*

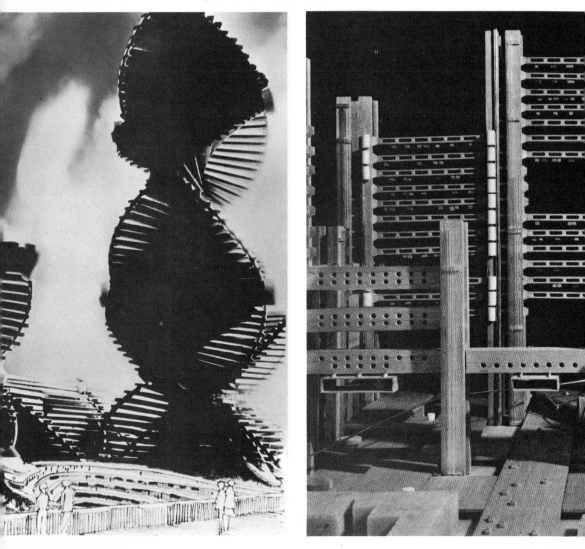

new ideas in urban accommodation, and judged by Kenzo Tange, produced a new wave of young graduates' designs in the idiom. More than one—including the first prize winner, Akira Shibuya, born in 1939—created artificial land on bridges spanning between service shafts (*Fig. 4*). A second place winner, Osamu Ishiyama, born in 1944, had an ingenious vertical cluster of houses spiraling jerkily around its service shafts. A twenty-two-year-old team of juniors in the architecture department of Waseda University won honorable mention with a system of interlaced beams stacked like a house of cards around a service core and ready to carry a variety of residential components on their cantilevered ends (*Fig. 5*). Characteristically, the designers noted that "the resident can select and partici-

5. *Waseda University junior team project, section, 1966.*

pate in the 'building' of the home in which he is going to live."

The next similar competition run by the same magazine in 1967 produced at the year's end another collection of related ideas which had moved a safe but satisfactory distance ahead. The winning entry this time was by a team of average age twenty-five—Kunihiko Hayakowa, Takagi, Koichiro Kimura, Katsuhiko Akimitsu—who replanned a central district running from Tokyo station out through a particularly congested area, turning it into a beautifully organized composition of horizontal latticework, residential wings punctured by funnel-topped communal spaces (*Figs. 6–7*). Rather to the disapproval of the assessor, Uzo Nishiyama, the young architects proposed a subtle architectural intrusion into family life. They increased the space for

6. *Kunihiko Hayakowa team project, plan and section, 1967.*

7. *Kunihiko Hayakowa team project, model, 1967.*

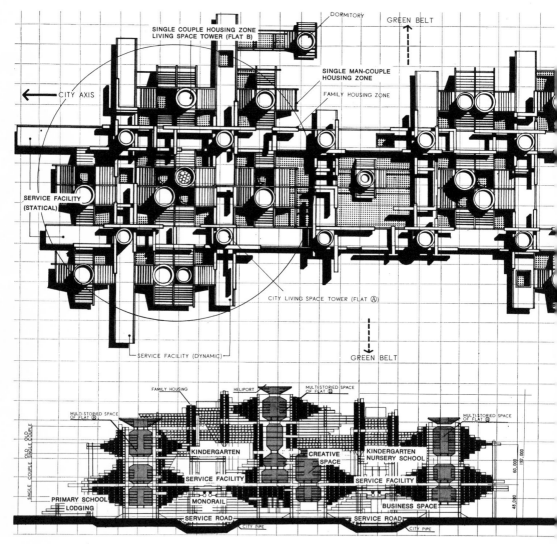

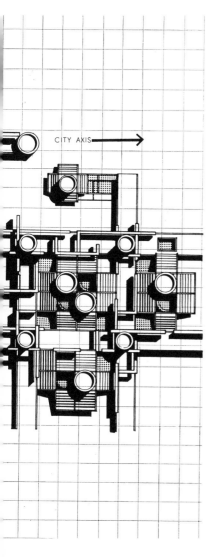

CITY AXIS ⟶

communal activities at the expense of private living rooms, leaving, however, some private room for what they described as the "three vital elements of human life: sleep and body development, evacuation and procreation."[2] Other entrants in the competition had not yet quite abandoned family living under the pressure of population. A number proposed comparatively formal dwelling cells, or free individual units, in various energetic revisions of and improvements on earlier Metabolist and Archigram themes. A remarkable number exploited the formal device of contrasting rectilinear dwelling platforms with vertical cylindrical service shafts—a Tange device, as we shall see. Stylistic influences of other established architects were apparent, and the Metabolist emphasis on allowance for growth and change was everywhere. The steady drift of Japan into the world architecture club was indicated by the fact that eight out of the hundred entries came from foreign countries, including the U.S.A., France and Mexico.

Despite its kinship to other movements, Metabolism is peculiar to Japan. Its main publications are available only in Japanese. As a group it may die but the influence of its concept already extends throughout Japan, far beyond the membership proper. One thing that distinguishes Metabolism from most other avant-garde movements throughout the history of modern architecture is that it is so little ahead of the Japanese establishment. The Futurists, Suprematists, Archigrams and others of Europe were protest movements, directed against a stodgy architectural profession as well as all other obstacles in society which blocked the way to the new world. The Metabolism movement could claim in Kikutake's Marine City (*Fig. 1*) a pioneer project as early as 1958, two years ahead of the publication of Tange's Plan for Tokyo. Compared with the average position in the West, the Japanese avant-garde has had to run hard to keep avant. The young rebels may mock the European fathers of modern architecture, and even criticize Le Corbusier, but rarely do they challenge the Japanese leaders. They seem to recognize that some of the most successful architects in the land are in the same boat with them, and that even if its sailing is painfully slow it is headed in a satisfactory direction.

The Metabolists and the Archigrams were always far apart in the matter of form. Western rebels have tended all through the twentieth century to reach through the purely technological to the science-fiction vision. The switched-on electric plug-in concept has some obsessed supporters in Japan, too, but on the whole the greater fascination for Japanese visionaries has been the structural and formal potentialities of the forthcoming artificial landscape. After Kikutake and Tange many have been captivated by the prospect of building over the water. Kikutake's second essay on the same theme, Ocean City of 1962, made all the buildings a play on the circle—

low disks and rings and high cylinders, all standing deep in the water with land left practically clear for nonurban pursuits (*Fig. 8*).

These water-borne schemes of Kikutake in many ways exemplify the new Japanese architecture. Putting the whole living environment out in the water reflects not only a desire to escape the crowded land; it provides architecture with a clean slate on which to build its new forms, and may symbolize young Japan's despair about the mess which previous generations have made of the urban landscape. In form, Ocean City is practically free of Le Corbusier's influence, being no less bold but much more disciplined, if by a fairly arbitrary geometrical theme. It is, however, proud of its flexibility within that

8. *Kiyonori Kikutake: Ocean City, model, 1962.*

discipline, which is expressed by the random disposition of the living cells, their snorkels combining to make giant nutmeg graters, which are threaded on straight service-core shafts. These shafts are crowned with construction cranes until they are fully encrusted with living cells. In such ways not only the structure but the technology and the methodology of the structure are celebrated visually in the architecture.

Finally, the spirit in which it is offered is typical of an earnestness which may lead to Japan's eventual discovery of the thing which its packed, progressive people will need before any others: the inevitable, but reluctant new kind of operating base for human society, the new kind of city. Kiyonori Kikutake has said that Ocean City is neither a suggestion of a technological possibility nor a proposal of an actual urban pattern. He presented it merely as a contribution to thinking about cities.

The Japanese architect is more conscious than most that man's total environment is involuntarily becoming more artificial all the time, and desperately needs the planner-architect, or architect-planner, to guide it so that the degree of artificiality inherent even now in a megalopolis like Tokyo may be bearable. The architect could bring flexibility, fluidity and visual order to the mindless growths. The Japanese architect needs to be, and would like to be, in the forefront of world developments to this end.

Yet in Japan as elsewhere the architect-planners have to do more than expend themselves on hypothetical schemes to convince the powers that be of their worth. The architect-planners of Japan have not, so far, been given adequate scope by the governmental authorities to test what they could do in reshaping the cities. An ambitious scheme of 1962 for transforming the Dojima district near the center of Osaka, by a bold rebuilding of four city blocks, was watered down by annual degrees until all the flavor had gone. The landowners who were affected would not cooperate and no governmental agency was prepared to compel them to do so.

Japan's architectural prophets have, with few exceptions, little honor in their own country. Most of their proposals and many of their works which have had a critical success internationally are by no means unconditionally endorsed by the authorities, no more than they are unequivocally loved by the people. The eternal, internal conflict which makes architecture so enigmatic to most laymen, the contest between art and technology, was never more apparent than in Japan today. The nation is inclined to be obsessed with advanced technology, largely because technology has done so much so quickly to change Japanese life. On the other hand, the bias of serious Japanese architecture always has been and still is to the left, to the artistic side, of a perfectly balanced position. Unlike the West, Japan has always held the design of functional objects to be a serious artistic matter, not really subservient to the fine or freer arts.

The most pronounced new direction in world architecture at this time may be said to be a new preoccupation with the requirements of people. Never before has there been so much talk about people in Western or Japanese architectural journals. The basic Functionalist approach of the twentieth century has passed through Machine-Functionalism to Programatic-Functionalism to what we might now call "Peopleism." To take the simplest of examples, a European Peopleist architect will smash a window through a wall anywhere, without hesitation, if he thinks people might like to look out at that spot. The Japanese architect is aware of this approach, of course, and of its validity under many circumstances. He, too, talks much about people, but he still retains a little more respect for the wall.

Of course, the old conflict between the two sides of architecture really interests laymen primarily; it never seems of much importance to a working architect. He knows it will never be solved and the best that can be done in any generation, in any region, is to produce a new definition of the terms of this intrinsic conflict of building. The Japanese layman, or client, or commissioner of architecture is, despite his recognition of the historical artistic role of architecture, as fearful as any Western client that art may somehow conflict with his architect's pursuit of the most efficient and economical technology to solve the problem at hand. But the Japanese architect sees no cause for fear. He cannot often afford to be as romantic as some of his race who are now Americans, but even if he could he doesn't want to fight the practical problems of living in Japan: the tight land and tight budgets, the galloping technology. To him his art of architecture consists of controlling these very things. He has visions, but he doesn't see them on a plane separated from the functions. To him the art of architecture includes the job of furnishing a function with a vision, so that the finished building impinges on the viewer or the occupier through all his senses with an integrated character, or essence. Yet it must be admitted that, to the influential Japanese layman—the rich industrialist, or the Government man who might order a new direction in urban reconstruction—even the most experienced architects appear to be still living in a tower. It is not an ivory one, admittedly, but in a way its raw concrete looks more untrustworthy than ivory to a wary investor or politician.

BETWEEN EAST AND WEST

DESPITE their failure to gain universal acclamation in their own country, the prophets of Japan's new architecture have produced an extraordinary surge of sophistication. A considerable number of them have stepped almost simultaneously into command of the modern building arts and technologies. This is quite a phenomenon. After all, even the warmest of Western Japophiles could not argue that the Japanese nation can claim equally high accomplishments in all the Western fields cultivated in the century since the Meiji Revolution. Japanese jazz, for instance, has neither the subtlety nor the crudity necessary to compete near the top level, Japanese dress is hardly exciting, and the famous Japanese variety shows are so determinedly international and impeccably polished that every trace of local character is rubbed off.

The one artistic problem that is peculiar to Japan is the nation's particular sort of insularity. Sensitive Japanese are both proud and awed by the feeling that they are neither of the East nor the West, but somewhere in between. "We huddle here as it were in a valley between the two worlds," wrote Kunio Mayekawa, the doyen of modern architects, in 1961, and he added: "We indeed find ourselves geographically situated in a good vantage point from which to observe the changing world situation."[3] That is the older man's voice. Many of the younger men do not judge their situation to be a valley and are not content only to observe. They feel swelling under their feet the third super power in the world. The hundred million people of Japan have lain low under the American defense umbrella since 1945, pleased to devote all their resources to industrial rather than to military strength. Their economy has grown into an adolescent giant that has not yet felt the need to test its strength, although it knows itself to be the third biggest in the world. Japan's automated industry uses more computers than any country except the United States, builds half the ships of the world as well as an impressive amount of electronic and precision equipment. Japan is the third producer of cars after the United States and West Germany and is fourth in the space race after the big two and France. And still its industry keeps expanding faster than any other in the world. In ten years, construction investment has grown to six times its original size and construction now accounts for twenty percent of the Gross National Product.

Yet in spite of the enormous prospects, for the present the ambivalent, in-between position brings to most creative people now at work, and especially to architects, a sense of isolation that can be frustrating. Despite jet planes and all modern mass communications the Japanese architect is cut off from his international colleagues by the most formidable differences of language and location. Naturally, successful Japanese architects travel, and many speak English, and all see the journals from the United States and Europe. But inevitably many of the leaders are cut off from the stimulation of close and regular intellectual exchange with colleagues who have a similar professional faith but different problems to solve. Ideas in Japanese architecture are thus inclined toward inbreeding, with both good and bad consequences.

The most notable advantage of working in a secluded cultural harbor is the comparative freedom from confusing quick changes in the winds of fashion. The busy worker is conscious only of the slow swell and retreat of the tides of style. It is this more than any other factor that has permitted Japan to develop such a consistent approach. Among the disadvantages is the comparative freedom from the pain of international criticism when a brave try falls on its face. The safe harbor accounts for some of the naïveté as well as the excitement in Japanese architecture.

The clients of architecture also are spared international scorn for misdemeanors. Rightly or wrongly, some Japanese architects think that there would be fewer acts of respectable vandalism if their country were less insular. They refer to the aesthetic destruction of Nara, the historic city which might have been a cultural capital but has been disturbed by handsome but impolite newcomers, like the Nara Prefecture Government Building. They think that the needless destruction of the central public rooms of Frank Lloyd Wright's renowned Imperial Hotel in Tokyo might never have been contemplated if Japan conversed more with America. They are probably wrong.

When the Japanese claims to be between East and West, he means it geographically, culturally and politically. Sixteen centuries or so of Asian development, with one century at the end turned toward Europe and America, has produced a vigorous neutrality in international relations, in politics and in art.

The style which Japanese architects have so rapidly evolved is also something of an in-between. It is not a compromise, but it is equidistant from Functionalism and Formalism, from Technocracy and Humanism. It is halfway between the integrated, unified "organic" architecture of Frank Lloyd Wright (as experienced firsthand in the master's Imperial Hotel) and the cool, hard, geometrical-abstract forms of Le Corbusier (as experienced firsthand in that master's museum at Ueno Park.) It exploits Le Corbusier's techniques—the raw planes of concrete, the superhuman scale—but in the best examples it derives from Wright and from its own background the love of a formal binding theme.

Formal themes are the nitroglycerin of architecture. If handled with sensitivity they can produce architecture of transcendental quality and power. If they are not they may explode in the architect's face. The fascination with formal themes led in the early days of the new Japanese architecture to some rather weird adventures, and for a time around 1960 the excesses of Japanese formalism were something of an "in" joke in the little world coterie of architecture-watchers. The strange shapes that caused raised eyebrows were not arbitrary. They were brainwave solutions to various architectural problems, usually passionately rationalized by their creators, to nobody else's great conviction. A late building, of 1965–66, which typifies the courage and calamities of this phase is the Miyakonojo Civic Center (*Fig. 9*) by Kiyonori Kikutake. It is a startling building that looks something like a giant, old-fashioned leather bellows extended to their utmost and about to be compressed again. It is rather disappointing to find that the structure actually has no moving parts. The bellows in fact are the side walls and vaulted roof over the main auditorium of the building. The "leather" membrane is steel sheeting, and it is straddled and supported by seven great steel U-shaped frames which fan out from a concrete base structure. Tension rods connect the frames externally, adding to the effect of movable bellows.

The architect rationalized this thoroughly ungainly design by explaining that he decided to divide the structure of the building into two parts, in accordance with Metabolist theory: the parts that may change and the parts that may not. The permanent sectors, or "fundamental spaces," such as the lobbies, cafés and seating tiers, he built as a sturdy concrete pedestal. The parts liable to be changed from time to time, such as the stage mechanism and the flies, he made of steel. The unlikely bellows-shape was the result of his attempt to give order to all the technical "inequalities." In shaping this single order, his aim was "the establishment of a humanistic nature."

To a great extent he achieved his aims. There is a sense of order, and it is no doubt humanistic in its flexibility and its attempt to relate the space inside the giant bellows to the human contents. It was a brave attempt. "But the problem is difficult," Kikutake confessed, "as work on this project showed us."[4] In fact, the joint between the permanent concrete and changeable steel was unresolved and their natures clashed. The giant bellows looked heavily contrived, an unconvincing throwback to European Expressionism and machine-worship of the 1920s, and perilously close to ridiculous. Yet this and other earlier unsuccessful experiments had validity and even in failure had value in the development of the new Japan Style.

If it is possible to select one building to characterize that style,

9. *Kiyonori Kikutake: Miyakonojo Civic Center, 1965–66.*

not necessarily at its most convincing but in its strongest imagery, the example must be the Kyoto International Conference Hall (*Figs. 43–44, pp. 62–63*). This is a big public complex by a lake, in a park seperated by a hill from the streets of Kyoto. Sachio Otani won the prize of being its designer in a competition against other star architects. He made a low, massive, horizontally stressed, compact but fragmented block. He enclosed it generally with precast concrete of a consistent grayness but in a lively variety of planklike shapes. The device that gave the whole its unity, drama and remarkable Japanese character was his choice of the trapezoidal form.

Every column that rises from the ground or out of the lake, every wall or balustrade, is angled inward or outward at twenty-two degrees from the vertical. Sometimes two inward sloping walls meet at a point reminiscent of the more ancient shrines' steep gables. Sometimes they form a V opening to the sky reminiscent of the crossed projecting rafters, called *chigi*, above the roof of an Ise shrine. The Japanese look is so intense it is suspected immediately by practically every viewer, and no one is more conscious of this than its architect. But Otani confidently defends it on rational grounds, as if the last thing he wanted was that it should look Japanese. Certainly, he admits, the device of slanting pillars is in the Japanese tradition, but it also occurs in European architecture, he says, "And we can scarcely call it really Japanese."[5]

He explains the real reason for his choice of the trapezoid to govern the cross-sectional form of the building. First there was the "layer system" into which the functional requirements fell: big requirements at the bottom, smaller on top. Then there were the internal considerations of the main hall. The trapezoid made a logical shape for an auditorium; sight lines were good, the space was widest at the bottom where it was most needed, the walls were out of parallel alignment to the improvement of the acoustics. Moreover, the trapezoid suggested a fascinating way of adjusting a room to the required size without affecting the structural framework: simply by raising or lowering the floor level he could create smaller or larger floor areas.

Meanwhile Otani organized the functional requirements of the complex by solving the problems in the separate parts and then bringing them together in a high-density spatial grouping. Now, since unity of conception is an essential part of the Japan Style, Otani, having tentatively adopted the trapezoid for the main spaces, felt obliged to carry it through. However, he reports, "When we attempted to fit some of the building's other functions into the form some illogicalities arose." He then thought of using an inverted trapezoid as well, and found that every function could be suited by one or the other. So he developed a dual system of spaces, interlocking, and bound together by the consistent structural angle.

Thus the suspect external image grew out of the inside requirements. At least this was true at the start. "I did not want to create a plan in which the whole regulates the parts," says the architect, "but one in which we go beyond the parts—which remain living things—to give birth to the organization of the whole." Yet it is also true that an image so strong as this one can take charge at times and may draw out its architect further than he intended to go.

The strength of the new Japan Style may be measured by the depth of its penetration through the generations of architects now practicing. As I have said, the avant-garde is in the same boat as the leaders, and, while there is still much bad commercial building, there is an extraordinary amount of agreement among those who are attempting serious architecture. Many of the visions of the youngest and brightest men look remarkably like Kenzo Tange's work. Antonin Raymond, the man who went to Japan with Wright to work on the Imperial and stayed on to practice, thereby making a major contribution to the early development of modern architecture, has now in turn absorbed influences from younger Japanese. Some of his recent works, like the Nanzan Seminary at Nagoya and a chapel at Rikkyo Primary School in Tokyo, are no longer sympathetic foreigners in Japan but part of the new mainstream of creative architecture.

As already mentioned, the architecture in this mainstream is not the only kind in Japan. Even in the field of sincere and serious architecture there are some rare aberrations like the ornamented art nouveau of Jun'ichiro Ishikawa's Insho Domoto Museum at Kyoto (Fig. 10). What the international world of architecture knows as the Japanese style, what the architecture-conscious tourist seeks out, what is illustrated in this book and in the self-congratulatory journals which Japan herself publishes so beautifully, represents only a narrow band of the building spectrum. It consists mainly of municipal buildings: city halls, culture centers, auditoriums, museums; a few university buildings, a very limited number of the richer houses, a tiny fraction of commercial and industrial buildings. And the architects responsible are only a small proportion of all the architects in Japan. That, nevertheless, is quite a quantity, for the total number of architects qualified under the Architects' Law is a quarter of a million, which means an average of one architect for every 400 people. In most Western countries the average is about one architect per 3000. However, there is no real translation in Japanese for "architect," and the term used for qualified architects, kenchikushi, includes two classes, A and B. Many in Class B might be better defined as architectural assistants or draftsmen in Western terms.

If one ignores, as is usual in these circumstances, the mass of careless and commercial building in the sluggish currents on either side and looks only at the main creative stream, then it is found that most things worth noting come from professional offices employing, all told, only about three percent of the architects in the country. The Japan Architects' Association, the highest professional group, has fewer than 800 members. A smaller proportion of good solid work comes from the better architects employed by the better construction companies.

The comparatively small creative leadership may be divided loosely into four generations or groups. First, the most prolific visionaries of Metabolist delights: the older students and younger graduates, the competition enterers. This group also includes the very youngest men in practice, like Hiroshi Hara, born in 1936, whose work is disturbing, challenging, promising, but as yet not mature enough to suggest a new direction (*Fig. 11*). Then the more settled

10. *Jun'ichiro Ishikawa: Insho Domoto Art Museum, Kyoto, 1966.*

practitioners: those now near the age of forty. They graduated after World War II and in most cases did not start independent practice until after 1960. This group includes dynamic, independent and busy men like Kikutake, Isozaki, Kurokawa, Otaka and Otani. They are the immediate inspiration to youth but it would be by no means correct to say that they alone are steering the new direction of the Japan Style.

The generation just a few years older, which graduated during the war and molded the new architecture on top of the ashes, is still a major creative source. It includes internationally respected architects like Hiroshi Oe, Yoshinobu Ashihara and Junzo Yoshimura. Kenzo Tange, who is popularly and critically recognized as the master of Japanese architecture, belongs in this group. Yet again, slightly older men close behind them, the pioneers of modern architecture before World War II, are also still a vital part of the movement. Kunio Mayekawa and Junzo Sakakura, the Le Corbusier pupils, continue to create prominent and powerful works; and Togo Murano, one who helped greatly to show a way toward a union of traditional and modern, still seems at the peak of his career at the age of seventy-seven.

There are, of course, many individual mannerisms to be seen and theories to be heard within each of these four groups, but nearly all reveal a philosophical and aesthetic kinship. The resulting style of Japan is simply accepted by the great majority of thoughtful architects as the genuine way to build.

11. *Hiroshi Hara: Sakura City Council Primary School, 1967.*

AMONG THE ARCHITECTS

IT MUST be repeated that the subject of this book is not all the modern architecture of Japan but only the Architects' Modern, or the new Japan Style. Even this narrower field obviously has been subjected to personal selection. I have deliberately excluded the more frantic and freakish exercises in form-mongering, as well as obviously experimental work, however diverting. I have concentrated on the more responsible and rational element. Even so, the field is wide; yet who does one select for closer examination and illustration? And, having selected some, in what order does one place them?

The following selection was made in an attempt to concentrate on those architects who by some nuance of theory or practice help most to define the new style. Most of them represent it precisely, but some deviate a little, and the deviations are just as important to our understanding of its limits.

Any short list must omit numerous men of equal ability and importance to some of those who are included. I am conscious, nevertheless, that that is a poor excuse for not spending more time on the work of such well-known men as Kiyoshi Kawasaki, Masaru Matsuda, Takeo Sato, Takamasa Yoshizaka (*Fig. 13*), the group which calls itself RIA (the Research Institute of Architecture; *Figs. 14–15*), and Hiroshi Oe (*Fig. 12*). Antonin Raymond is omitted only because he was not Japanese born, if that can be counted as fair under the circumstances. The Ishimoto Architectural Office and several others like it which are part of some constructional or industrial organization do much work of high quality in fine Japan Style. They are an important factor in Japanese architecture, for their work usually is incomparably better than the products of anonymously employed architects in the West. However, they can hardly be included in a selection such as this, for the team changes from time to time while the name remains and the identity of the creative member is always obscure.

Then, in what order does one place the selected men? Priority by age may be invidious. Alphabetical order seems particularly inappropriate when dealing with translations from the Japanese. So I shall start with some of the Metabolist generation, pass to an anti-Metabolist, then to the older men whose influence is still vital, and finally to a leader of modern world architecture.

12. *Hiroshi Oe: Mexican Embassy, Tokyo, 1964.*

13. *Takamasa Yoshizaka: Gotsu City Hall, Shimane Prefecture, 1960.*

14. *Research Institute of Architecture: Shinseisakuza Cultural Center, the theater, 1967.*

15. *Research Institute of Architecture: Shinseisakuza Cultural Center, the pool, office, and dormitory, 1966.*

KIYONORI KIKUTAKE

As the number of earlier references to him might suggest, Kiyonori Kikutake is one of the leaders of the younger generation. He is now, in fact, one of the most successful forty-year-old architects in the world, with an international reputation very rare for one of his age. Success has come to him in one decade.

He graduated from Waseda University with a degree in architecture at the age of twenty, and one in engineering two years later. For a time he worked in established offices, including that of Murano and Mori. He first came to international notice with the publication of one of his first buildings—a house of modest dimensions for himself. It had, however, such bland simplicity and masterly conviction that the world seemed to recognize immediately that a strong new talent was budding here. He called it the Sky House, *(Figs. 16–17)*. It was simply one open square room with the plumbing compartments appended on two sides, the whole wrapped by a veranda and held high above the ground on four pylons.

For the next five years his reputation grew on the basis of his philosophy rather than on completed buildings. At the age of thirty-two he was one of the younger panelists at the 1960 World Design Conference in Tokyo and led the formation of the Metabolism Group. He built little, but he published the many notable visionary city drawings already mentioned, and soon the doors to the conferences of the international architectural fraternity were opened to him. He won the seventh annual Pan-Pacific Prize from the Hawaii Chapter of the American Institute of Architects in 1964 (Kenzo Tange won the first in 1958) and spoke both at a convention of the California Council of the A.I.A. and at a summer arts festival in Finland.

His most productive period began in 1963 with a building that fulfilled his promise, and justifiably was well publicized after winning the Architectural Institute of Japan's prize for the year. It was a "treasure house" built to replace a temple building of the Izumo Shrine that had been damaged by fire *(Fig. 18)*. Kikutake designed it as a long, tall space with evocative inward-sloping walls *(Fig. 19)*. These he made of massive, spaced horizontal slabs of concrete through which the light filtered—in by day and out by night. Its form, space and structure placed this building in the middle of the new Japan Style, but certain qualities in the treatment made it a personal Kikutake essay.

First, he was fascinated by texture. Instead of the usual raw concrete, the building presents almost too many intricacies and variations of surface treatment in precast concrete.

Second, Kikutake demonstrated in this building what he de-

16. *Sky House, Tokyo, 1958.*

17. *Sky House, living room.*

scribes as his basic three-step methodology. The first step is *Ka*, or the conceiving of a sense of spatial order, an image. The second is *Kata*, or the technological system which grows out of the order, and which can be applied to various situations and functions. The final step is reached when the system produces *Katachi*, or the characteristic formal quality to be sensed in the particular building.

Third, in accordance with Metabolist theory, Kikutake freed some parts that are liable to change from the rigid discipline of the main structure, which is presumably unlikely ever to feel the need to change (*Fig. 20*). Thus the office section is almost an independent construction slipped loosely inside the main space and not blocking completely the long view down each side. Also, auxiliary functional elements, like the stairs, porches and rooms with plumbing, are freely and tenuously attached externally. One especially large Metabolist excrescence on one side of the building carries a stair and alcove under a strangely twisted and temporary-looking roof. It was a proud demonstration of Metabolist principle, but so jarring aesthetically that it is rarely shown in photographs of the building.

However, the Metabolistic changeable part of the Miyakonojo Civic Center of 1966 could not be avoided by photographers (*Figs. 9, 21–22*). The metal bellows-like form which has already been described dominates the whole building. The photographers take their pictures grimly, but they seem embarrassed by the bellows. This is the building where Kikutake's work, and his Metabolism, struggle furthest out from the central stream of Japanese architecture. It was not a great success popularly, critically, nor apparently in the eyes of its own architect. Kikutake had let his head run away with his heart: the theory or *Kata* was convincing; the practical result or *Katachi* was disturbing. But Kikutake will return to the problem again with nothing lost by this adventure.

18. *Great Shrine of Izumo, administration building, 1963.*

Meanwhile, he built a spectacular hotel in which Metabolist principles were less in evidence than traditional references and a clear display of the structural and functional elements. It was the Hotel Tokoen at Yonago City, completed in 1965, and he carried the top half of a functionally fragmented façade on tall slim columns grouped in fours and tied together with concrete beams. This was an adaptation in concrete of a traditional timber technique called *Nuki*. On top he built a penthouse with a twisted roof. It produced a silhouette of entirely modern geometrical curves, yet in conjunction with the straight lines below they presented a peculiarly Japanese image.

His Pacific Hotel at Chigasaki in 1967 was essentially conventional in concept for a resort hotel: a modest tower block rising from a free spread of public spaces (*Figs. 23–24*). The whole design approach, however, from the stuck-on external bathrooms of the residential tower to provisions for growth and improved techniques in the plant room was obsessed with the problems of changing conditions. Indeed, Kikutake's main contribution to date is his effort to solve the problem of changing conditions—both during design and after construction—without losing sight of a binding total image. He writes: "Unlike the architecture of the past, contemporary architecture must be changeable, movable and comprehensible architecture, capable of meeting the changing requirements of the contemporary age. In order to reflect dynamic reality, what is needed is not a fixed, static function, but rather one which is capable of undergoing metabolic changes. Therefore, naturally, our ideas about architecture are also bound to change. We must stop thinking in terms of function and form, and think instead in terms of space and changeable function."[6]

19. *Great Shrine of Izumo, administration building, interior of treasury.*

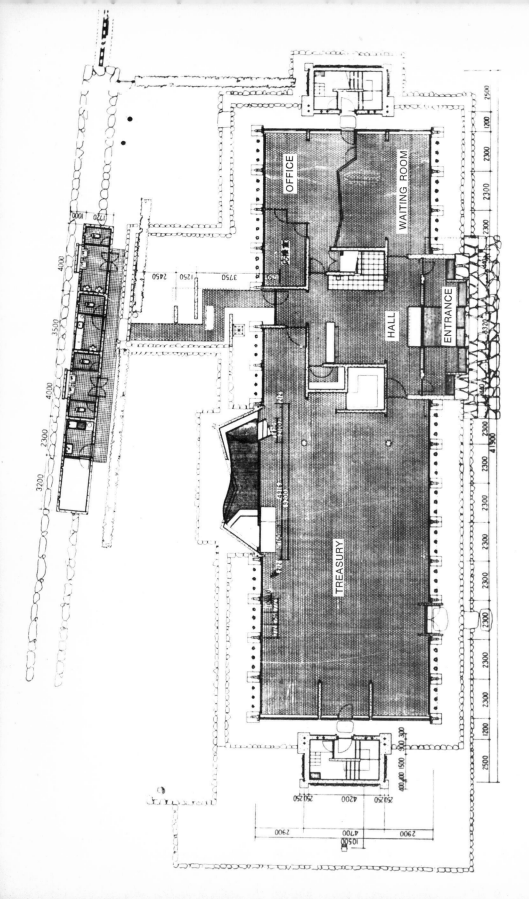

20. *Great Shrine of Izumo, first floor plan of administration building.*

21. *Miyakonojo Civic Center, 1965–66.*

22. *Miyakonojo Civic Center, interior.*

23. *Pacific Hotel, Chigasaki, 1967.*

24. *Pacific Hotel, Chigasaki. Above, plan of first floor; below, plan of fifth to eighth floors.*

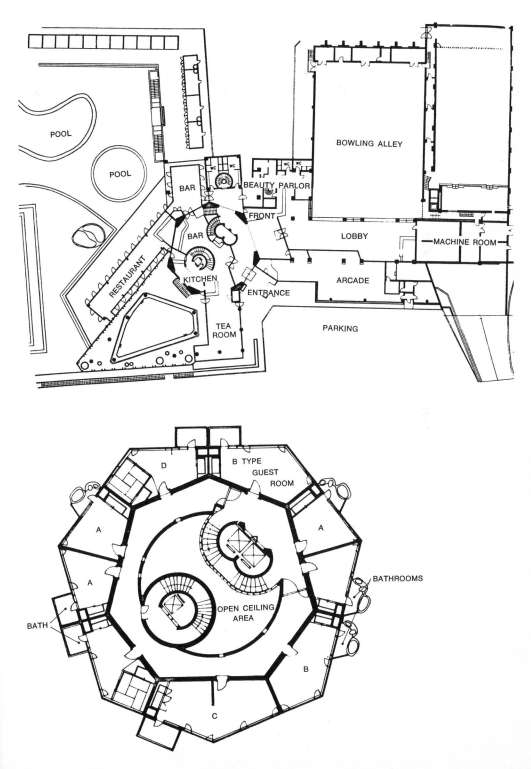

POOL

POOL

BAR

BEAUTY PARLOR

WC WC WC

BOWLING ALLEY

FRONT

BAR

RESTAURANT

KITCHEN

TEA ROOM

ENTRANCE

LOBBY

MACHINE ROOM

ARCADE

PARKING

D

B TYPE GUEST ROOM

A

A

A

B

C

BATH

OPEN CEILING AREA

BATHROOMS

NORIAKI KUROKAWA

If the metaphysics behind Metabolism sometimes seems inscrutable and rather overblown in relation to the concrete examples to be seen so far, this is mainly due to Noriaki Kurokawa, one of the originators of the group and its most impatient member. He has become its most verbose spokesman—prolific, often brilliant, and frequently unintelligible—he has been described as an *enfant terrible* and an angry young man (born in 1934). Most galling is that he once was known as the "paper architect."

All of this is because his natural talent is more inclined to be constructive than theoretical, but he was driven to over-theorizing by circumstances. He was only twenty-six, and just three years out of Kyoto University, when he helped to found the Metabolism Group. He worked in the Kenzo Tange Laboratory at Tokyo University, but for some years received no commissions as an independent architect. Thus his ardor was turned to theoretical writing and to the paper architecture of unsolicited spectacular city planning and housing schemes.

His theorizing involves a seemingly endless number of sub-concepts to Metabolism. For instance, "infra-structuring" which he describes as "the method that attempts to see architecture and cities as information patterns and to compose their structures in keeping with this interpretation." The lack of sharp imagery here is not simply the result of language difficulties. His colleague in the foundation group of Metabolism, Noboru Kawazoe, admits to the confusion but writes: "Not everything he says deserves disregarding." Kawazoe advises: "The reader should not be taken in by the words but should feel the theory behind them."[7] And when it suits him, Kurokawa can come down to earth and to mundane material details, as when he gave quite precise specifications on how to design a Metabolist building:

1. Divide the spaces into basic units.
2. Divide the units into equipment units and living units.
3. Clarify the difference in metabolic rhythms among the unit spaces.
4. Clarify the connectors and joints among spaces with differing metabolic rhythms.[8]

Kurokawa uses the expressions "Porous Spaces" and "Fiber Form" to distinguish between two recurrent formal themes in his designs. They are not inconsistent nor complementary forms, just different, and he seems to select one or the other pragmatically according to which works best for the problem at hand.

Porous Spaces he describes as heterogeneous, metamorphic, membranous and spatial. In effect they are usually cluster designs, like his Helix City scheme of 1961 already mentioned (*Fig. 3*), and several other visionary schemes of about the same time. He calls them animal-like forms.

Fiber Form, on the contrary, he sees as plantlike, for it grows in linear trunks and branches instead of clusters.

As he turned thirty in 1964, and more and bigger commissions began to arrive in his office, both design systems were applied to actual buildings. The Porous Spaces system appeared in a factory for Nitto Foods, a city hall for Sagae and a pleasureground: the Yamagata Hawaii Dreamland. Fiber Form appeared in two apartment blocks, and is conspicuous in some of his latest works, notably the Aichi Prefecture Welfare Center (*Fig. 25*) and the Goshikidai Recreation Village lodging house. Both these buildings have residential wings sprouting out like spring growth from pruned trunks which contain all the communal living and serving facilities. Kurokawa's admiration for Louis Kahn is in evidence in the fashionable exploitation of the diagonal in the residential wings.

He shows himself not to be above international fashion again in the Yamagata Hawaii Dreamland building (*Fig. 26*), the most successful and original of his Porous Spaces. This building takes the shape of a distorted ring, enclosing a pool and housing games facilities and restaurants (*Figs. 27–29*). Sprouting from the ring, both inside and outside—in an animal-like rather than plantlike way—are cylindrical towers carrying stairs and services. These Tange-like cylindrical towers display on the surfaces the broken ribbed technique introduced by Paul Rudolph at Yale in 1964. However, Kurokawa is a young man of quite sufficient talent (some call it genius) to rise above the tricks of fashion and the abstruse argument which still tends to obscure his contribution.

Two of his most impressive buildings so far are simple pavilions in the National Children's Land at Yokohama: the Memorial House of Hans Christian Andersen and the central lodge (*Figs. 30–32*). Neither has a visible trace of Metabolism nor any other metaphysical theory. Both are simply practical, sensible, serenely composed and self-contained buildings; progressive and direct in structural concept yet with a strong scent of the tradition. In short, they are beautiful examples of the mainstream of the new Japan Style.

25. *Aichi Prefecture Welfare Center, under construction, model, 1968.*

26. *Yamagata Hawaii Dreamland, 1967.*

27. *Yamagata Hawaii Dreamland, pool.*

28. *Yamagata Hawaii Dreamland, play area.*

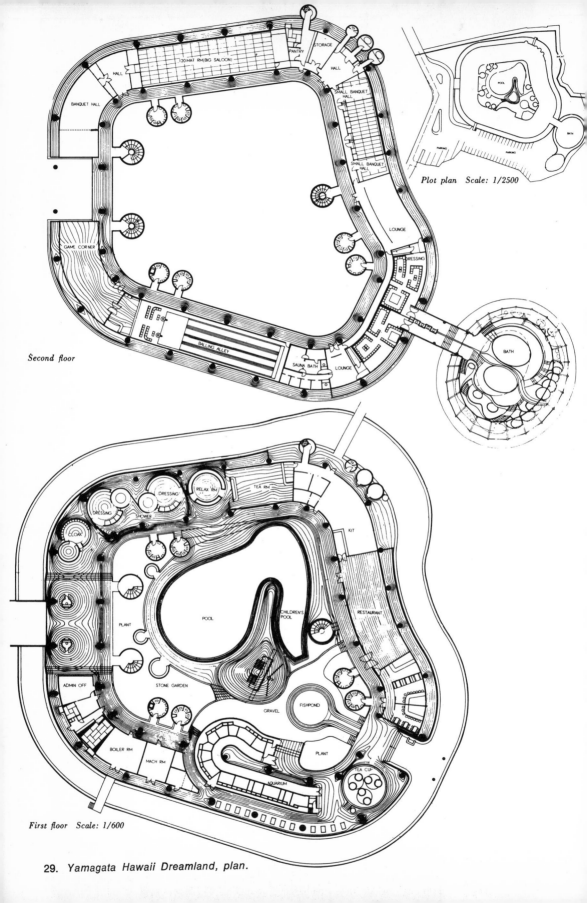

Plot plan Scale: 1/2500

Second floor

First floor Scale: 1/600

29. Yamagata Hawaii Dreamland, plan.

30. *National Children's Land, central lodge, Yokohama. 1965.*

31. *National Children's Land, central lodge entrance.*

32. *National Children's Land, central lodge, rear view.*

MASATO OTAKA

In the work of Masato Otaka, a foundation member of the Metabolism Group, the two great incompatible qualities of architecture appear: romanticism and realism. He seeks to balance them, which may be the ultimate goal of architecture, and displays them both at about equal strength. Unfortunately, he rarely achieves them simultaneously in a single building; some of Otaka's buildings are sternly realist and some whimsically romantic.

At forty-five, Otaka is one of the older Metabolists and one of the first to succeed, founding his own office in 1961, the year after the group was formed. In much of his work, even today, there is evidence of his long apprenticeship before that: twelve years in the office of Kunio Mayekawa. During that time he directed, among other works, perhaps the earliest triumph of the new Japan Style: Mayekawa's Tokyo Metropolitan Festival Hall. Reflections of that powerful building still appear in his designs.

As a young Metabolist he duly produced visionary solutions to urban planning problems, including at least one over the water—another floating city in Tokyo Bay. This occupied a lot of water for the sake of a three percent increase in Tokyo's accommodation. It demonstrated the romantic Otaka, while in another proposal for Ohtemachi, a rather dismal area beside the main downtown center of Marunouchi, he appeared as the pure realist (*Fig. 33*). He planned a podium, or new building level, raised 12 meters above ground with parking and car access roads below, all to be provided by the Government. Then, private interests would be sold the new elevated "land" for their own independent buildings, to be controlled by certain general restrictions. He developed this "urban platform" theme again in a scheme for Sakaide City (*Fig. 34*). It was not a startlingly new concept, and was positively stuffy compared with some of the more excited soaring or sunken schemes of full-blown Metabolism.

Unexpectedly, his romantic side shows more clearly in most of his completed buildings. His Chiba Prefectural Central Library of 1968 has almost Gothic proportions in its elaborately contrived prestressed concrete system. Each tall column stands perversely not under any beam of the floor or roof grid overhead, but in the center of a square of beams, equidistant from all of them. The column thus has to spread out on top like a capital. In Otaka's Yamanouchi Agricultural Co-op Union Hall, the massive concrete beams are not simply overshot a meter or so beyond their last point of duty, which is commonplace, but their ends are curved in an almost grotesque allusion to the tradition (*Fig. 35*).

Otaka likes to compare the way an architect designs with the way Newton came up with the law of gravity. Before the architect's apple of an idea falls and the guiding vision for the building flashes upon him, there must be a long preparatory study of the problems in order to build a set of circumstances in which the right idea will suddenly crystallize. He is a dedicated artist, convinced that the architect can only justify himself in modern society if he has abundant creative ideas and individuality. Yet, as Otaka sees it, the individuality should express itself within a team or group. To the three dimensions of space, Sigfried Giedion adapted to architectural theory the concept of time as a fourth dimension. Otaka proposes a fifth one: "the dimensions of the group." By this he means not only designing for the group—for society, for mass participation in architecture—but also designing *by* a group.

He seeks to achieve both objectives by a system of organization in his office team designed to build up orderly sets of circumstances fertile to ideas. Thus, for instance, he subdivides the team thinking on any design problem into three groups, each concentrating on a different scale range. One group limits its work on the drawing boards to small scale, say 1 to 3,000, at which a house is a mere spot, forcing attention on to broader problems of the social environment. A second group hunts for architectural ideas at conventional architectural drawing scale, and a third concentrates on details and

33. *Ohtemachi project, model, 1963.*

the nature of materials by virtue of working only at scales from 1 in 50 up to full size.

Every sizable architectural office in the world faces the problem of internally organizing to achieve a coordinated team effort. Conventionally, the object is to make the work of all the different consultants, specialists, designers and draftsmen look as if it had come from one mind and one pair of hands. But is this the only possible aesthetic rule? Maybe a new architecture which gave visible evidence of the number of different minds and hands involved would be more valid. From Bauhaus days onward Walter Gropius has advocated selfless teamwork to produce a pure anonymous unity. Otaka's concept of Group-form is quite different. He would not stifle the prima donnas; his group could contain a number of them and could allow each a separate area of operation. A single building might include a variety of differing forms and expressions, an urban landscape even more; and they could be changed at any time without any fear of upsetting an established theme.

Group-form is an aesthetic extension of the Metabolism creed. For any real chance of success the idea clearly demands a project of some dimensions, and perhaps the actual works, as distinct from the visionary schemes, of Masato Otaka's office have not yet been big enough in scale. In some, like the Chiba Prefectural Culture Center, the space is crowded by an overabundance of ideas, including twisted walls, random tile patterns, scatter lights and several variations on Paul Rudolph's ribbed concrete (*Fig. 36*). The anti-unity concept of the Group-form idea is a challenge to traditional architectural values, of both West and East, at least as radical as Functionalism was in its time. In the West it has been called more frivolously Action Architecture. Some examples of Group-form might be called Mob-form, or even Sample-room Style.

34. *Urban platform apartments, Sakaide, 1968.*

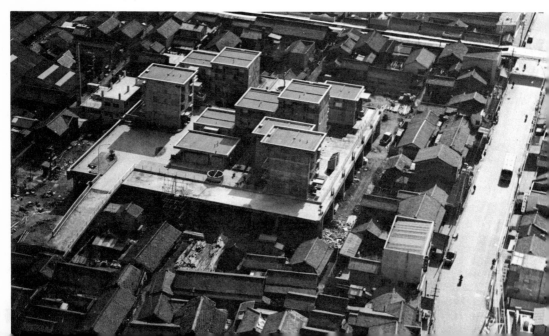

35. *Yamanouchi Agricultural Co-op Union Hall, 1966–67.*

36. *Chiba Prefectural Culture Center, 1967.*

FUMIHIKO MAKI

Much of Masata Otaka's early theoretical work was done in conjunction with a man five years younger, Fumihiko Maki, another member of the original Metabolism Group and the one with the closest links to the West.

After graduating from Tokyo University, Maki studied at Cranbrook Academy, was for a time Assistant Professor of Architecture at Washington University, and worked for Skidmore, Owings and Merrill, and later for José Luis Sert at Cambridge, Massachusetts. Back home in Japan he worked with Tange before starting his own practice. In 1960 when Metabolism was founded he collaborated with Otaka in inventing the concept and the term "Group-form." In the same year he acted alone as architectural consultant to the Takenaka Constructing Company for the Toyoda Auditorium at Nagoya University (*Fig. 37*). Even allowing for the fact that the construction company relieved him of a good deal of the technical worries, it was an extraordinarily mature design for a man barely in his thirties. He enclosed the big main hall in a long heavy-lidded box, far too large for it, but with fascinating and usable open spaces packed around it under the lid.

During 1965–67 his own office, Maki and Associates, was responsible for the site planning and the building design of a complete

37. *Toyoda Auditorium, Nagoya University, 1960.*

new campus for Rissho University at Kumagaya, near Tokyo (*Figs. 38–40*). The various structures—classrooms, lecture theaters, gymnasium, dormitories—were spread at low density; the academic buildings grouped around an irregular L-shaped, multilevel, brick-paved plaza (*Fig. 41*). The buildings were placed with a traditional sense of delight in the long vista and the unexpected blind spot and the surprise around a corner (*Fig. 42*). Yet delight is not in the Metabolist vocabulary. Maki sought a flexible system or framework of spaces which would remain valid and inviolable throughout the life of the university—during every phase of the four-stage construction program which he himself would control, and even after that when others might add new elements to the group. His own buildings were reserved, gray with touches of orange, unified to an extent by a care for consistency in details of openings, lighting, balustrades and equipment. They were anticonceptual buildings, each taking its own form, uncoordinated by any geometrical or structural theme. But the campus as a whole was not without theme.

The concept that tied the building masses together was in the organization of the space between them. This organization was helped by a rhythm of "stations" or square spaces of moderate size for students' casual meetings, bulletin boards, posters, and so on. These stations were sometimes outdoors, enclosed merely by walls, and sometimes interior rooms (or, in the language of Metabolism, "interiorized outdoor spaces" and "exteriorized indoor spaces"). Outside the stations, buildings were left free to adopt any practical mass and form. Each might almost have come from a different architect's office. This, in short, was Group-form in practice.

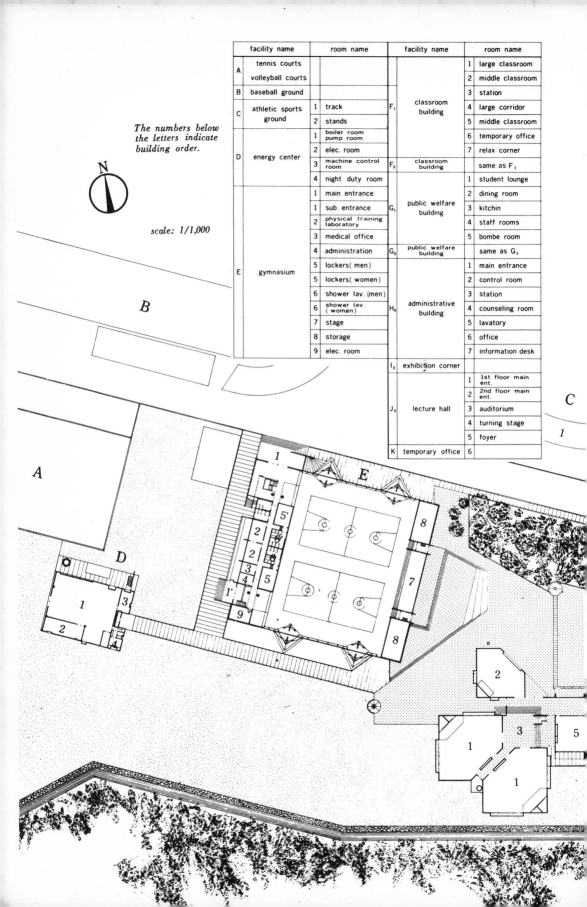

The numbers below the letters indicate building order.

N

scale: 1/1,000

facility name		room name		facility name		room name	
A	tennis courts			F₁	classroom building	1	large classroom
	volleyball courts					2	middle classroom
B	baseball ground					3	station
C	athletic sports ground	1	track			4	large corridor
		2	stands			5	middle classroom
D	energy center	1	boiler room pump room			6	temporary office
		2	elec. room			7	relax corner
		3	machine control room	F₂	classroom building		same as F₁
		4	night duty room	G₁	public welfare building	1	student lounge
E	gymnasium	1	main entrance			2	dining room
		1	sub. entrance			3	kitchin
		2	physical training laboratory			4	staff rooms
		3	medical office			5	bombe room
		4	administration	G₂	public welfare building		same as G₁
		5	lockers(men)	H₂	administrative building	1	main entrance
		5	lockers(women)			2	control room
		6	shower lav. (men)			3	station
		6	shower lav. (women)			4	counseling room
		7	stage			5	lavatory
		8	storage			6	office
		9	elec. room			7	information desk
				I₂	exhibition corner		
				J₂	lecture hall	1	1st floor main ent.
						2	2nd floor main ent.
						3	auditorium
						4	turning stage
						5	foyer
				K	temporary office	6	

B

A

D

E

C

1

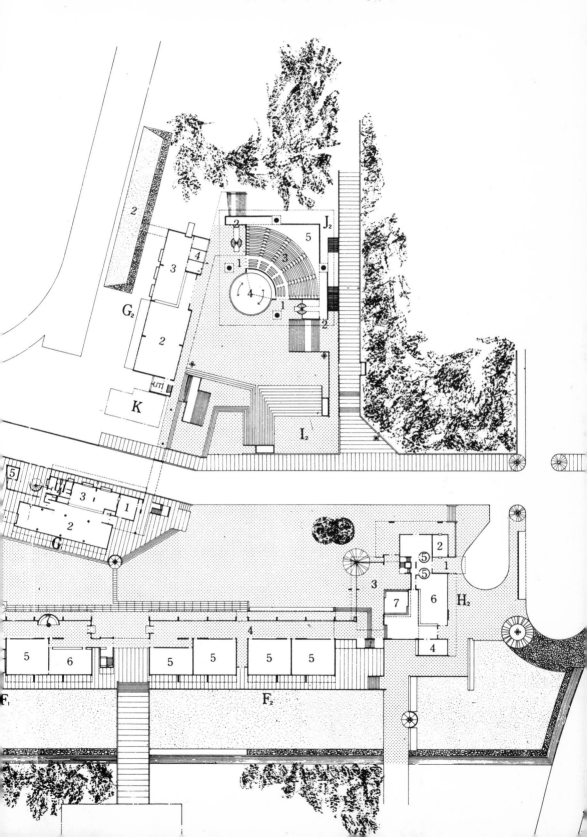

39. *Rissho University. Left, lecture wing; center, gymnasium; right, student union.*

40. *Rissho University. Left, lecture wing; center, gymnasium; right, student's facilities.*

41. *Rissho University, the central plaza.*

42. *Rissho University, spinal corridor of the lecture wing.*

SACHIO OTANI

Born in 1924, Sachio Otani is a year younger than Otaka and their names are sometimes linked as dynamic members of the generation following Kenzo Tange's. Otani was a member of Tange's Architectural Research Institute for many years after his graduation from the School of Architecture at Tokyo University. Perhaps because of the stronger influence of Tange on him his work has a firmer conceptual quality that distinguishes it from most of his contemporary Metabolists and sets it in quite another category of architecture from Otaka's Group-form works.

In the summer of 1963 Otani was placed first, ahead of 194 other competitors, in an open national competition called by the prefecture for the International Conference Hall in Kyoto (*Figs. 43–44*). That building of multiplane walls canting in and out, reeking of traditional allusions that are disowned by Otani, has already been described (page 30). It has a sudden, violent visual impact, an utterly uncompromising image. One must love it or loathe it at first sight. Not all his other works are as single-minded as that, but he is driven by a sense of order and unity even in his Metabolistic urban visions.

His Kojimachi project (*Fig. 45*), for instance, was a disciplined scheme for high-density family living which preserved privacy and

43. *Kyoto International Conference Hall, 1963–65.*

encouraged social intercourse by means of a hierarchy of court-yards: first a small private court for every family, then semipublic places for neighbors to meet and children to play, finally central parks for the use of the whole community.

In his Children's Hall at Shibuya, Tokyo, 1964 (*Fig. 46*), and the sprawling headquarters of a cult known as the Tensko Kotai Jingu sect at Tabuse district, Yamaguchi (*Fig. 47*), designed in conjunction with Taneo Oki and finished in 1966, the image is less intense. Artistic cohesion is still the objective, but it is achieved not so much by the strict repetition of a motif as by a sculptural massing of bold forms in a uniform material. These buildings are a remarkable achievement, a heterogeneous complex of big and small seminar halls, living quarters and offices, in a rural, hilly setting. It is held together by the consistency in the handling of a practically irreducible set of materials: concrete walls, timber panel linings, *tatami* floors.

In the charming development called Children's Land at Nara-machi, Kohoku Ward, Yokohama, where several architects of his generation have produced sensitive work within a master plan designed by Takashi Asada, Otani built in 1967 a playground known as the Juvenile Hall (*Figs. 48–49*). Apart from sand piles, pools and play equipment, the architectural function was to provide some enclosed and some semienclosed spaces to extend the children's play-time in imperfect weather. In these structures Otani (with help from two other designers, Masao Tanaka and Koichi Fujita) produced a beautiful combination of orderliness and playfulness. The ground

44. *Kyoto International Conference Hall.*

plan is quite severe. Steel columns were set out on the *en-tout-cas* paving at about 8-meter intervals in equilateral triangular formation, and each triangle was roofed independently but identically with a tapered vault of cor-ten steel—that is, an arch on one side of the triangle receded to nothing at the point opposite that side. The playfulness entered with the random placing of these vaults, sometimes turned against each other to open crescent-shaped views of sky, sometimes grouped with six points together to make a round-edged hexagon, which might even claim resemblance to a cherry blossom. The random openings cast a lively shadow. Moreover, the horizontal ladders that formed the structural beam edges to the triangles and the tension rods that tied free edges together were all designed deliberately to invite climbing and hanging.

45. *Kojimachi project for high–density courtyard dwellings, model, 1961.*

46. *Children's Hall, Tokyo, 1964.*

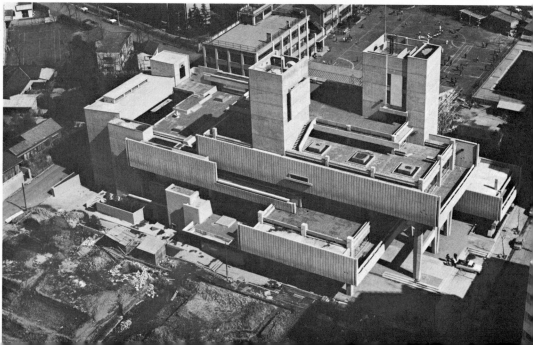

47. *Headquarters of the Tensko Kotai Jingu sect, Tabuse district, Yamaguchi, 1966.*

48. *Juvenile Hall and playground for Children's Land, model, Yokohama, 1967.*

49. *Playground at Children's Land, shelters.*

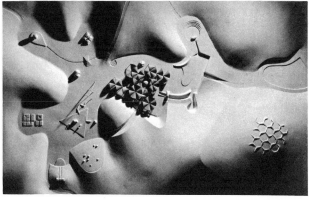

ARATA ISOZAKI

The Oita Prefectural Library at Oita City is a comparatively small building of enormous presence (*Fig. 51*). Its initial visual impact is almost like a physical blow. Giant concrete beams made with a hollow square section project meters beyond the enclosing walls and even find their support at times far away from the business of building. The approaching visitor looks down the menacing square muzzles of four such huge concrete cannons. He rises eleven wide corner steps to a podium, crosses a ramped concrete bridge 15 meters long, and enters directly to the core of the building. He is in a hall at second floor level, two tall stories high, 38 meters long and barely 9 meters wide. It is broken in the center by a circular concrete-walled browsing area and spanned across midspace by a concrete bridge (*Fig. 53*). The long side walls of this hall are double and they secrete the stairways that lead up to offices and down to book storage. The main reading room and some minor spaces are found beyond the double walls (*Fig. 52*). In the minor spaces the staple gray of concrete gives way to primary colors on painted burlap which covers walls and ceiling.

This library of 1962–66 was the first major commission granted to Arata Isozaki, and he made it a tour de force. It moved his colleague, Hiroshi Hara, to panegyrize Isozaki as "the first really creative architect to appear in this country."[9]

There is no doubt that Isozaki is a brilliant young man (born in 1931) and that the Oita Library has many fascinating qualities, including inventive forms, convincing structural expression, and a reassuring sense of order behind the startling forms and colors. The Western architect to whom it is most closely related is Paul Rudolph, yet without having any of his ribbed concrete which is so popular elsewhere in Japan. The relationship with Rudolph comes from the combination of orderly, geometrical plan and free, open cross-section. Like Rudolph, Isozaki aims to produce unexpected, impressive and expressive spaces, exploiting contrasts of height and scale, changes in levels, vertigo, color and chiaroscurist devices. Like Rudolph, his methods are sometimes delightfully arbitrary.

The influence of Tange is also written clearly in Isozaki's work. He graduated from the architecture department of Tokyo University in 1954, aged twenty-three, and went to work under his professor on the Kenzo Tange research staff. While taking an M.A. in 1956 and a Ph.D. in 1961 he worked on such famous Tange projects as the Plan for Tokyo of 1960. Isozaki published a drawing of his own, dated 1960, illustrating a scheme for rebuilding a subsection of

Tokyo. It showed office blocks elevated high above traffic ways and constructed as beams spanning between cylindrical service shafts (*Fig. 50*). It suggests the existence of a feed-back influence on Tange's own later work.

In 1963, he opened his own office, calling it the Arata Isozaki Atelier. He felt his way capably and strongly in a highschool (*Figs. 54–55*) and a house of 1964, but it was not until he built the Oita Library in 1966, followed closely by a tall, blind, angulated bank nearby (*Fig. 56*), that he gave visual notice of his aim to create simultaneously powerful, orderly form and diverse, emotive spaces— even, if need be, at the expense of logic.

50. *Space City project, model, 1962.*

51. *Oita Prefectural Library, 1962–66.*

52. *Oita Prefectural Library, reading room.*

53. *Oita Prefectural Library, browsing area.*

54. *Girls' High School, Oita, 1963–64.*

55. *Girls' High School, Oita.*

56. *Bank at Oita, 1966–68.*

KIMIO YOKOYAMA

The Taisekiji Temple at Fujimiya City, at the base of Mt. Fuji, was established centuries ago as headquarters of a Buddhist sect. After World War II the Soka Gakkai, a new sect of much power, took control and sponsored a series of major monumental buildings in the precincts of the great old temple. These include a treasury and great hall, meeting halls, rest halls and most recently a lodging house to accommodate the staggering number of at least 12,000 pilgrims who visit the temple daily. The building program has extended over a period of some thirteen years, since the days when the new Japan was tentatively finding its feet after the war, and the main phases through which Japanese architecture has passed since then are mirrored in the buildings. They were all designed by one man, Kimio Yokoyama.

Each building at the temple is brilliant of its kind. Yokoyama came to Taisekiji in 1955 after a stint as chief designer at the Matsuda and Hirate Architectural Office following his graduation from Waseda University. His early buildings reflect the European or Le Corbusier influence. The Dai Kyakuden, a building of 1962, represents the break away when Japan began seeking her own expression within the international movement (*Figs. 57–58*). The immediate influence at this time was Kunio Mayekawa. His work is directly reflected in this building in a series of upswept balconies faced in precast pebblefaced concrete.

The lodging house, of 1966, reflects Metabolism (*Fig. 59*). This is a big building. The floor area of the first section is 3,033 square meters and two more sections of equal size are planned (*Fig. 60*). Yet the functional program was simple in the extreme. Pilgrims are spartan and require merely a few huge rooms for community sleeping on the floor, and some communal toilet facilities. However, the bland simplicity of the interior facilities and planning could never be guessed from the exterior of this building, which displays a dynamic complexity of projections and recesses, panels and voids and hooded vents, bolts and brackets. It is not a criticism of Yokoyama to say that he has made a simple building look complicated. It may be our eyes that are seeing wrong. He deliberately set out, in direct reaction against the bandbox look of modern commercial-industrial building, to show every element of the building, structural and functional—or, perhaps like a stage magician, to *appear* to show every element.

He chose to use prefabricated concrete structural members and wall panels throughout, because of the great deal of repetition, and to make the floors by the lift-slab method. The building was thus assembled from thousands of dry parts and bolted together. This logically resulted in numerous joints and protuberances on the exterior surface. These no doubt could have been cunningly concealed, but Yokoyama clearly relished every one of them (*Fig. 61*). He also put the columns outside and of course the elevator and stairwells and toilet wings. He held the water tanks on semicircular cradles triumphantly high above the roof. And in a final gesture of pure Metabolistic faith he even placed the rows of prefabricated cylindrical shower stalls half in and half outside the building (*Fig. 62*). They present, externally, a bold and quite decorative fluting. This device may be open to criticism on the grounds of its overenthusiastic celebration of a minor function of the human routine, but no other single architectural detail has so clearly demonstrated to the world the essence of Metabolism.

57. *Taisekiji Temple, the Dai Kyakuden (Grand Reception Hall), Fujimaya City, 1962.*

58. *Taisekiji Temple, the Dai Kyakuden.*

59. *Taisekiji Temple, the lodging house, 1966.*

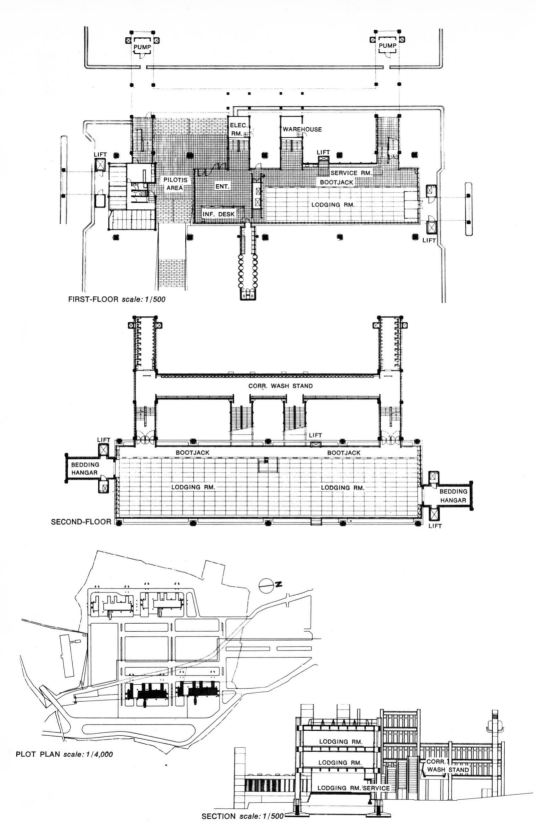

FIRST-FLOOR scale: 1/500

PUMP

PUMP

ELEC. RM.

WAREHOUSE

LIFT

PILOTIS AREA

ENT.

SERVICE RM.

BOOTJACK

LODGING RM.

INF. DESK

LIFT

LIFT

SECOND-FLOOR

CORR. WASH STAND

LIFT

LIFT

BOOTJACK

BOOTJACK

BEDDING HANGAR

LODGING RM.

LODGING RM.

BEDDING HANGAR

LIFT

PLOT PLAN scale: 1/4,000

N

SECTION scale: 1/500

LODGING RM.

LODGING RM.

CORR. WASH STAND

LODGING RM. SERVICE

60. Taisekiji Temple, first and second floor plans, site plan and section of the lodging house.

61. *Taisekiji Temple, general view of the west side of the lodging house.*

62. *Taisekiji Temple, exterior view of shower room, lodging house.*

KAZUO SHINOHARA

Kazuo Shinohara has built only a few small houses which look rather conventional from the outside. Sometimes they are made of traditional materials, including timber, tiled roofs and *shoji*; sometimes they are more evidently modern, in concrete with flat roofs. They are always clearly ordered and precisely detailed, but so unobtrusive that they slip quietly into the gray suburban wasteland and retire almost unnoticed behind the web of wires.

The importance of Shinohara lies in two facts: that these houses, indoors, are startlingly, movingly beautiful, and that he is the most eloquent advocate of the diffused, uncertain elements of anti-Metabolism.

He is not a conservative. He was a mathematician before he became, in 1962, Assistant Professor of Architecture at the Tokyo Institute of Technology. Born in 1925, he is of the age of many in the Metabolism Group and is as respectful of science and as awed by technology as any of them. Yet he has a touch of romanticism or humanism that resists the influence of Metabolist thinking when it narrows down to the house.

"I would like the houses I make to stand on this earth forever," he says with no immodesty. "I devote my interest to human hope and wish to produce things that will last forever."[10]

He admits that equipment changes over the years, as do accommodation requirements in the life of any family; yet he is confident that the identity of the house as a work of art transcends these minor practical matters. If a house is beautiful, families will adjust to it, and others will after them.

For years he has been saying that a house is art, and lately he has amended this to "houses have become art," as if to try to hurry disbelievers to convert. Indeed, in view of the onrush of technology and the logic of the Metabolists' stand, he argues that art is the only justification left for the existence of the single custom-built house. By art he means a quality in the house that touches the heart, and since domestic architecture touches the human existence so intimately, he cannot understand why it has not always been recognized among the finer arts. Actually he thinks it may be the finest of all, with the most "total link" to the human emotions.

The medium of the residential art, as he sees it, is "abstract expanses" or "symbolic spaces," and the basic spatial arrangements of his houses are impeccably orderly. One which he describes simply as a "House in White," has an exactly square plan under a pyramidal roof supported by a central pole which rises through a two-story living room (*Fig. 63*). This room occupies two-thirds of the house.

The remainder consists of two identical low-ceilinged bedrooms, one on top of the other, and a bathroom apologetically intruding in one corner (*Fig. 64*). The windows with their *shoji screens* are either low, on floor level, or high against the ceiling. They and the walls and ceiling are white. The round pole, cutting through the tall living room off-center, is a polished cedar log. It gives the essential emphasis to the height, and is a typically Japanese understated contrast, providing a unique quality to the bleached space.

Shinohara's most original contribution so far is a very small house built in 1967 for a documentary-film producer and his scriptwriter wife. At first sight the whole house seems to be no more than a slightly irregular room (*Fig. 65*) of about 50 square meters with a shed roof overhead and a low bathroom and kitchen partitioned off along the high side. A plain pine ladder resting against the partition gives access to a platform over the bathroom, where the owners may sleep if they wish. The walls are painted vivid red and black and the floor is compacted earth from which sprout, like mushrooms, beautiful, if unresilient laminated timber chairs and a dining table, all designed by the architect. Earth, he explains, is the theme of this building. In one corner of the room a stair drops down into the ground (*Fig. 66*). It leads to the main bedroom, which is not a cellar beneath the exposed house but a separate, underground extension of it beneath the garden which can be glimpsed from the main upper room. The result is weirdly beautiful, a deliberate reaction against pragmatic Functionalism and Rationalism and Metabolism. Shinohara believes it is the responsibility of the architect to protect and encourage human emotional activity in the face of industrial materialism. He also wants to escape from the rut, from all stereotypes, both old and new. Within a framework of respect for materials and spatial-structural purity, he frankly seeks "dynamic illogicality."

63. *House in white, living room, Suginami-ku, Tokyo, 1966.*

64. *House in white, first-floor plan.*

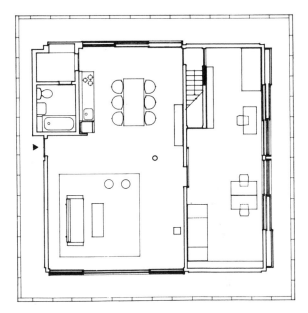

65. *House with an underground room, ground level room, Nerima-ku, Tokyo, 1967.*

66. *House with an underground room, section.*

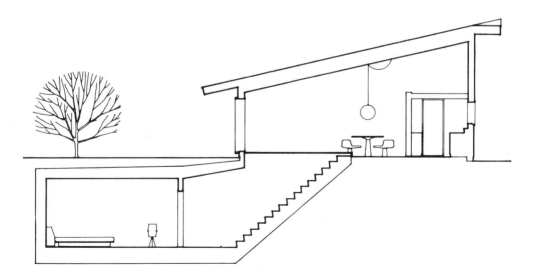

YOSHINOBU ASHIHARA

At this time the world probably knows Yoshinobu Ashihara best by a lighthearted example of his work, one of the most successful of the national pavilions at Montreal's Expo 67 *(Figs. 67–69)*. It was a structure of immediate visual impact and the only modern building at Expo that really needed no flag or name over the entrance to tell the visitor which country it represented. It was based on the image of the traditional *Azekura*-style Japanese log cabin, but it was in three sections, at three levels, the highest well clear of the ground, and logs which were extraordinarily long, prestressed concrete beams *(Fig. 68)*. Square in section and metal-tipped, they were prefabricated in Japan and shipped to Montreal; they overshot each other when they crossed at the corners, not by a few centimeters as is traditional, but by three meters or so. They were built up, crisscross, without notching, like a miniature doll's house made of matches, the wide gaps between them letting some sun in by day and colored light out by night. Apart from the disappointing interior—not by Ashihara—it was an amusing building and just right for Expo, but it gave little indication of the more serious work which Ashihara has been consistently performing in Japan since he started practice, in 1956, at the age of thirty-eight.

Ashihara knows the world well. He entered Harvard on a Fulbright Grant in 1952, just ten years after graduating from the University of Tokyo. With his Master's degree from Harvard he worked for a while in Marcel Breuer's firm in New York and then visited Europe on a Rockefeller Grant. He has since traveled frequently and in 1966 was a Visiting Professor at the University of New South Wales, Australia.

His big, busy practice now includes civic halls, cultural centers and university buildings, like most others in the mainstream of the new Japan Style, but it probably extends a little further than most of the others into the commercial field. His Sony Building of 1966 competes at night with the bright lights of the Ginza district, glowing from within in bands of color seen through a fine comb of aluminum louvers *(Fig. 70)*. The surface treatments in this case are far removed from the tough raw concrete that is the staple material of the Japan Style, for Ashihara thought it appropriate to give this building the same sort of machine precision that marks the famous Sony products. To this extent the building is atypical, but behind the aluminum comb it demonstrates a principle of spatial organization that recurs throughout Ashihara's work.

He is fascinated with the manipulation of functional space and has exploited the split level in numerous variations. The main function of the Sony Building is to display the products, much as in a department store (*Fig. 71*). The site was irregular, but Ashihara cut off the lumps and left himself with a square for the showrooms. He divided this square into four smaller ones and split the levels between all of these small squares so that each was about one meter higher than the one to its left, and was connected to it by a short flight of steps the full length of the square (*Figs. 72–73*). Thus the squares spiraled up, like a square Guggenheim Museum, but around a single solid column rather than an open well. There are twenty-seven of the small square platforms, making a "dimensional promenade" as the Sony advertising people say, or a "continuous interior space," as Ashihara prefers to call it.

He first used split or skip levels as a device for unifying interior space in the Chuo-Koron Publisher's Building in Tokyo in 1956. Again, two years later, in the Hotel Nikko he made the lobby and dining room of double height, but half sunk into the ground and entered at a half level. Thus he managed to squeeze an extra floor out of Tokyo's then tight height limit law. Later in the Kagawa Prefectural Library of 1961 and the Fine Arts Building of Musashino Art University, he played more with the idea. Always it was evident on the outside, for he deliberately encouraged broken horizontal lines to imply what was going on inside.

In 1960 Ashihara traveled through Europe again especially to study how the masters of all eras integrated interior and exterior space, and this integration became a major preoccupation. In 1962, he published a book, *Exterior Space in Architecture*, and at the same time was given what he considers his most significant commission in his first ten years of practice. This was the Olympic Gymnasium, control tower and grounds at Komazawa Park. For the first time he had the opportunity to integrate indoor and outdoor design on a large scale. Later, in a clubhouse for the Nihon Yusen Company of 1964, and the Ibagari Prefectural Culture Center of 1966 (*Figs. 74–75*), he subjected the whole building site to the medium of architecture. That is, in place of landscaping he gave the open areas a full architectural treatment with walls, brick paving, pools, changes of levels and materials—perhaps too many materials.

In the studios at Musashino Art University of 1963, Ashihara experienced his most successful adventure into space so far. He arranged eighteen square studios and eighteen square open spaces of the same size in a large random checkerboard and lifted the whole grid above the ground on sturdy pilotis (*Figs. 76–77*). Students can walk and talk and sit, and see right through the space underneath the big square building to other reaches of the campus. For half the time the floor of a studio hangs low and solid overhead and for the other half a shaft of daylight floods the paving and one can look up to the sky.

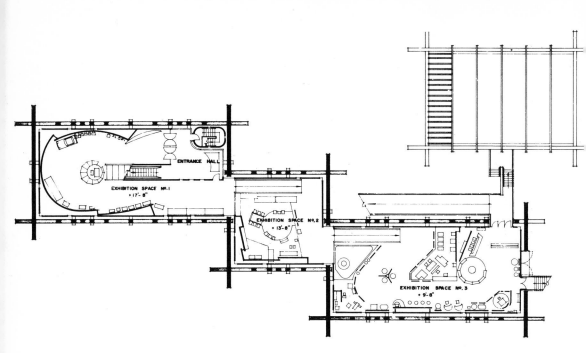

67. *Japanese pavilion at Expo 67, Montreal, plan.*

68. *Japanese pavilion at Expo 67, section.*

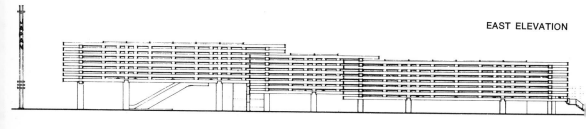

EAST ELEVATION

SOUTH ELEVATION

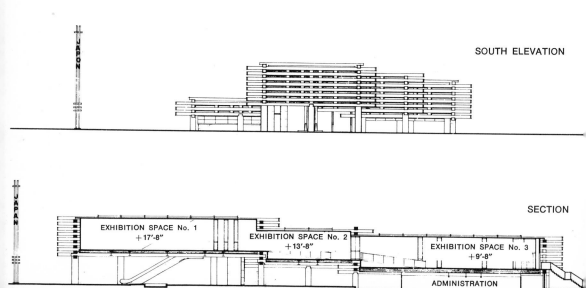

SECTION

EXHIBITION SPACE No. 1
+17'-8"

EXHIBITION SPACE No. 2
+13'-8"

EXHIBITION SPACE No. 3
+9'-8"

ADMINISTRATION

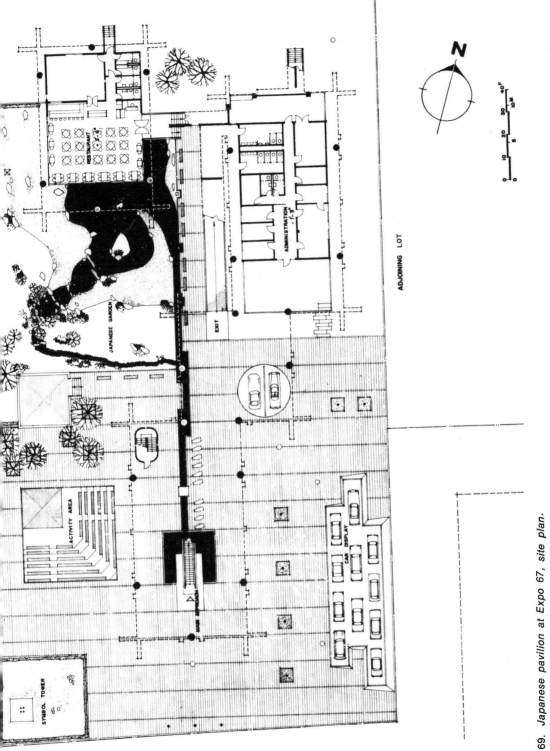

69. *Japanese pavilion at Expo 67, site plan.*

70. *Sony Building, Ginza, Tokyo, 1966.*

71. *Sony Building, showrooms.*

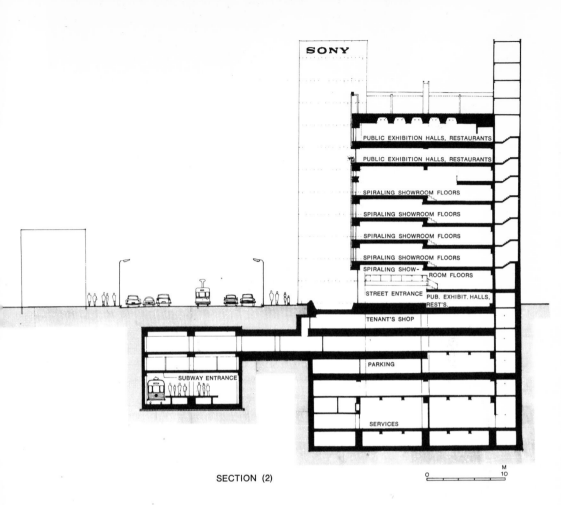

SONY

PUBLIC EXHIBITION HALLS, RESTAURANTS

PUBLIC EXHIBITION HALLS, RESTAURANTS

SPIRALING SHOWROOM FLOORS

SPIRALING SHOWROOM FLOORS

SPIRALING SHOWROOM FLOORS

SPIRALING SHOWROOM FLOORS

SPIRALING SHOW-
ROOM FLOORS

STREET ENTRANCE   PUB. EXHIBIT. HALLS, REST'S.

TENANT'S SHOP

SUBWAY ENTRANCE

PARKING

SERVICES

SECTION (2)

0   10 M

72. *Sony Building, section.*

73. *Sony Building, plan of third to sixth floors.*

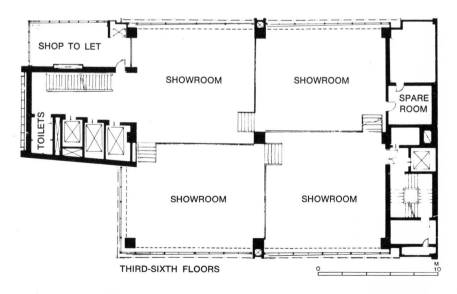

SHOP TO LET

TOILETS

SHOWROOM

SHOWROOM

SPARE
ROOM

SHOWROOM

SHOWROOM

THIRD-SIXTH FLOORS

0   10 M

74. *Ibaragi Prefecture Cultural Center, 1966.*

75. *Ibaragi Prefecture Cultural Center, plaza seen from the museum wing.*

76. *Studios at Musashino Art University, 1963.*

77. *Studios at Musashino Art University, detail.*

JUNZO YOSHIMURA

Junzo Yoshimura, born 1908, is like his buildings: gentle, gray and impeccably civilized. He and they represent a subtle blend of traditional and modern that erases international cultural boundaries not so much by drawing the modern West into Japan as by disseminating the Japanese essence into the modern West.

Fate has carried him into specialization in a building-type which is not common in Japan. He designs big, rich, private houses, and so sensitively and beautifully that his practice extends to the United States as well as into the Imperial Gardens. There, in the process of erecting a new palace for the Emperor, he ran afoul of bureaucrats. They must be almost the only people in the world who cannot admire the calm, controlled precision of his methods.

He often uses the traditional techniques of *shoji* screens and a *tatami* mat module for room sizes, while providing air-conditioning and a generous sprinkling of bathrooms. When he builds in timber, the style moves in close to the timeless Japanese domestic tradition, despite the loose chairs and beds (*Fig. 78*). When he builds in concrete, the traditional quality is less obvious because he does not imitate timber forms. Yet it is still present because he somehow manages to use reinforced concrete in the way one imagines that the ancients would have used it if it had been available to them: strongly, directly, modestly (*Figs. 79–80*).

Nothing could be much further from Yoshimura's serene and complete spaces than a dynamic new-directional movement like Metabolism, with its unfinished fingers clawing at the future. Yoshimura's direction is as old as the shrines, yet it is a persistent one, and even the rebels respect it and are affected by it, consciously or unconsciously.

The Yoshimura art is exemplified in the additions he made in 1966 to a famous old inn in Kyoto, the Hotel Tawaraya. Behind a three-story façade so reserved that it merges with the old part of the hotel and all but disappears behind the posts and wires of a busy Kyoto street, he created an oasis of calmness. Rooms turn inward to courtyards (*Fig. 81*). Each guest suite has, in the usual pattern of new Japanese style hotels, an eight-mat Japanese room (*Fig. 82*), a Western room, as well as a modified Japanese bath. Apart from the loose furniture, it is hard to say where Yoshimura Japanese ends and Yoshimura Western begins.

78. *House at Ikedayama, interior, Tokyo, 1965.*

79. *House at Ikedayama.*

80. *House at Ikedayama, interior.*

81. *Tawaraya Inn, Kyoto, 1965.*

82. *Tawaraya Inn, Japanese room.*

JUNZO SAKAKURA

The very first indication to the Western world that Japan might one day produce a twentieth-century style of its own was given more than thirty years ago. The hint was the Japan pavilion at the 1937 World Exposition in Paris (*Fig. 84*). It won a grand prix and left a lasting impression on modern architecture. It was a comparatively small building of two stories made of steel, glass, concrete panels and other new materials, but built with a delicacy and sensitivity that had hardly been seen before in modern architecture. It was of the Japanese tradition, but seen in a new reflected Western light. And now, a whole generation later, its architect, Junzo Sakakura, is still a leader of the Japan Style and one of her busiest practitioners.

Sakakura built the 1937 pavilion a year after returning to Japan following six years with Le Corbusier, during which time he had become chief of the master's studio. He is still known as the leading Japanese exponent of the Corbusier idiom and is proud of it. Yet that pavilion could not have been designed by Le Corbusier and very few of Sakakura's more recent buildings look like the later work of Le Corbusier. This puts them poles apart from the many Western buildings that directly reflect the forms and finishes invented by the master.

If Sakakura insists with old-fashioned Japanese modesty that he is nothing but a shadow or slave of Le Corbusier, one must suppose that he should know best. Nevertheless, his work gives no convincing evidence of it. Certainly he absorbed early from his patron the lesson that technological and structural engineering advances should be exploited not for their own sake but for the greater glory of the architectural art, which consists of putting emotive spaces around people. But his work is so much more gently persuasive than Le Corbusier's. It is strong but not furious; it has none of the artistic protest of his master's. Compare, for instance, Le Corbusier's and Sakakura's attitudes to the environment. When Le Corbusier added a building to Harvard he battered his way in between the Georgian red brick with a magnificent concrete flail. When Sakakura adds to a building, as at the Kamakura Museum of Modern Art in 1966 (*Fig. 83*), his first thought is to the final harmony of the environment which he is disturbing, and his personal expression is moderated accordingly.

These days, Sakakura is a respected senior of his profession and President of the Architectural Association of Japan. The works produced in the name of his organization exhibit a range of precise and appropriate expressions which no doubt reflect the many talents in his two big offices in Tokyo and Osaka.

At his Osaka Youth Outdoor Activities Center (*Figs. 85–86*), in the mountains, two hours away from downtown Osaka, an isolated knot of irregular, white concrete walls is roofed with random-pitched tiled roofs and peppered with small random windows as by a shotgun. The style is Mediterranean.

In the Kanagawa Prefectural Office Building, a conference hall, smaller conference rooms and offices are contained within a fourteen-story, meticulously polished slab which gives only subtle hints to the changes of interior functions (*Figs. 87–89*). The style is sophisticated commercial-international.

For a house of 1967, the Bhrwani residence, stripped-white cubist concrete holds huge slideway screens of plate glass (*Fig. 90*). The style is an old friend, the International Style, beautifully reproduced like a deliberate period revival.

In the Hiraoka City Hall wide bands of balconies are capped by a large overhanging, dished concrete roof (*Fig. 91*). The approach is straight down the middle of the new Japan Style.

The latest and biggest work of the Sakakura office is the Shinjuku Station Square in Tokyo (*Fig. 92*): a public place with a bus terminal, parking, roadworks and buildings, including a big department store—"Odakyu." The identity of the many smaller parts is satisfyingly acknowledged, but despite an obvious effort at organization the whole is incoherent. The elements enjoy a rather strained polygamous relationship to the dominating department store. An opportunity to create the larger-scale unity which Tokyo cries for was somehow missed. In the many aspects of this complex work most of Sakakura's earlier idioms are reflected, but the new Japan Style prevails.

83. *Kamakura Museum of Modern Art. Left, main building, 1951; right, annex, 1966.*

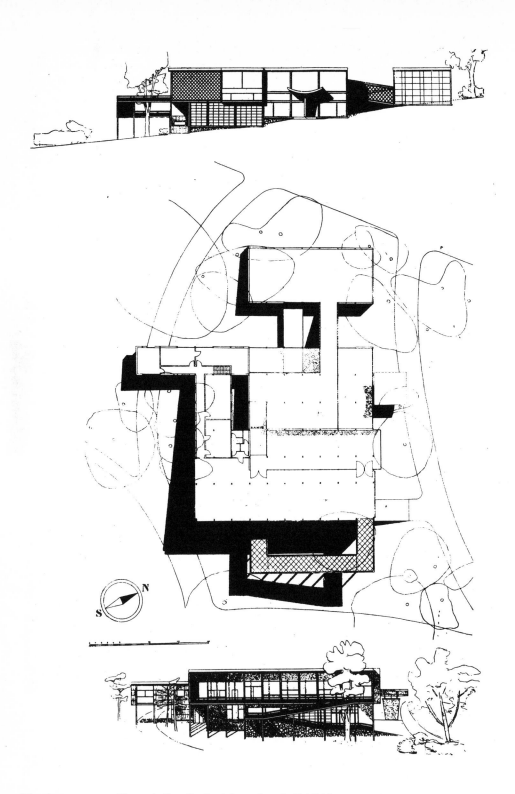

84. *Japanese pavilion at the Paris International Exhibition, plan and elevations, 1937.*

85. *Osaka Youth Outdoor Activities Center, 1966.*

86. *Osaka Youth Outdoor Activities Center.*

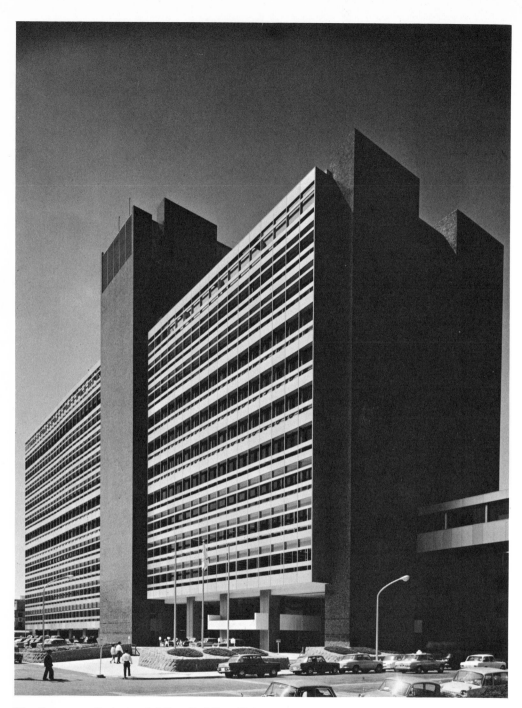

87. *Kanagawa Prefectural Office Building, Yokohama, 1966.*

88. *Kanagawa Prefectural Office Building, detail.*

89. *Kanagawa Prefectural Office Building, plan of seventh floor.*

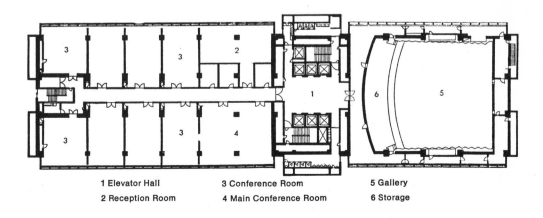

1 Elevator Hall   3 Conference Room   5 Gallery

2 Reception Room   4 Main Conference Room   6 Storage

90. *The Bhrwani residence, Kobe, 1967.*

91. *Hiraoka City Hall, 1964.*

92. *Shinjuku Station Square and Odakyu Department Store, Tokyo, 1967.*

KUNIO MAYEKAWA

The phenomenon of the new Japan Style began with the 1960 decade and was first isolated in the Tokyo Metropolitan Festival Hall, completed in 1961 (*Fig. 93*). Its architect, Kunio Mayekawa who, like Sakakura, was a pupil and disciple of Le Corbusier, has already been noted as the doyen of Japanese Modern and is at least twenty-five years older than many of the young practitioners. Yet it is often hard to differentiate between his and their works on grounds of vitality, strength, or style. Some of the most advanced young men are not too proud to adopt devices invented by Mayekawa about 1960.

The Metropolitan Festival Hall first displayed the new richness, the gargantuan dimensions and the allusive curves that declared their independence from the European approach. Before it, in the period of postwar reconstruction, Mayekawa had worked in almost undiluted Corbu style, notably in many austere, multistory apartment blocks. The Festival Hall marked a new expansive mood not only for him but for the nation as a whole. Around 1960 Japan felt it had the essential public works under control and began to extend itself again. The prefectural governments turned to a competitive race for culture centers—or concert halls with exhibition areas—and the first one, the Tokyo Hall, directly influenced many of them. Since these culture centers were always key community buildings, the subjects of keen study and discussion by citizens, they helped greatly to disseminate the new approach—the concrete and curves and massive Expressionism—across the nation.

Mayekawa has maintained an impressive output in the same idiom through the years, yet when he himself tackled the problem again later, in the Saitama Prefectural Culture Hall of 1966, he solved it in an entirely different and new way (*Fig. 96*). He realized that the previous halls were often monuments to their architects posing as monuments to the community. In the new building he deliberately subdued the solid forms and emphasized the spaces between them. He thus provided a kind of intimate urban square that is practically unknown in Japan. But he made the square an esplanade on several levels and he paved it with a bricklike ceramic tile similar to a tile he used on the wall surfaces, so that the outdoor space remained architectonic and never landscape (*Figs. 94–96*). It was very different from the early Mayekawa style, but in some ways a maturation rather than a renunciation. And he left some areas of raw concrete untiled, as if in nostalgia or in loyalty to an old love.

93. *Tokyo Metropolitan Festival Hall, 1961.*

94. *Saitama Prefectural Culture Hall, esplanade, 1966.*

95. *Saitama Prefectural Cultural Hall, esplanade view from the roof.*

96. *Saitama Prefectural Cultural Hall, foyer for large auditorium.*

TOGO MURANO

At the age of seventy-seven, Togo Murano could hardly be expected to be forging a new direction for Japanese architecture, yet he still has a hand on the steering wheel. This is because he represents the quality of Expressionism that is always present somehow in the Japan Style, even when the architect denies it and can prove mathematically how rational he has been.

Murano was an established architect long before World War II. He was versed in the traditional styles but was gradually drawn to the European Modern. After the war he returned to prominence with the rather ambiguous Memorial Cathedral for World Peace at Hiroshima, completed in 1955. In partnership with T. Mori after that, he has maintained an impressive output of thoughtful design. Not all of this is Expressionistic. Most of his early work was straight European Modern. Some, like his 1957 Sogo Department Store in Tokyo (*Fig. 97*), is sound spectacular-commercial, while his New Kabuki Theater in Osaka (1958) has a whimsical pagoda-like façade which claims justification from nearby Osaka Castle and the traditional plays which it shelters (*Fig. 98*). His tall office building for the Chiyoda Insurance Company in 1966 introduced cast aluminum as a facing material (*Fig. 99*).

But Togo Murano is clearly happiest when he forsakes the rational, the traditional, and the industrial and uses his sensitive imagination to create pure Expressionistic spaces in the Gaudi–Mendelsohn mood.

The theater inside his Nissei Kaikan Building beside the Imperial Hotel, Tokyo, has free-form walls of mosaic tiles curving weirdly to accommodate openings and throwing light over their top on to a dark, pebbly, Gaudian ceiling (*Fig. 100*).

His Takarazuka Catholic Church of 1967 appears to be straight out of a Mendelsohn sketchbook. Its long side walls of scratched, coarse, colored mortar converge on the sacristy, above which rises a spire some 23 meters high. The copper roof with its wide upturned brim sweeps in a slow wave down the nave to the base of the spire and then, carrying its protesting timber ceiling with it, shoots skyward up the hollow spire (*Figs. 101–102*). The forms are purely emotional and antistructural, and have thus been criticized in Japan. Yet a vision of emotive space as created here is always somewhere at the back of the mind of the new Japan architect, and Togo Murano's work will continue to influence it.

97. *Sogo Department Store, Tokyo, 1957.*

98. *New Kabuki Theater, Osaka, 1958.*

99. *Chiyoda Mutual Life Insurance Company office building, side view of clubroom, 1966.*

100. *Theater in the Nissei Kaikan Building, wall and ceiling detail, Tokyo, 1963.*

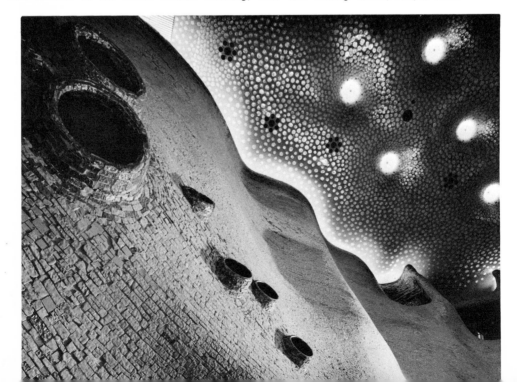

101. *Takarazuka Catholic Church, spire, 1967.*

102. *Takarazuka Catholic Church, wall detail.*

KENZO TANGE

Once or twice in a decade a building is constructed somewhere that hits the world architectural fraternity in the middle of its vision and changes the course of the art. Le Corbusier's Ronchamp Chapel, Eero Saarinen's Kresge dome at M.I.T., and Louis Kahn's Richards Laboratories were such buildings. Each seemed to crystallize an attitude and an approach which, for better or worse, had been in the air for some time without anyone actually realizing it until they saw it so crystallized. The Yamanashi Press and Radio Center at Kofu, seventy-five miles inland from Tokyo, built between September 1964 and November 1966, is another such building (*Fig. 114*). No other anywhere has so sharply caught the most advanced architectural spirit of the sixties as this gray citadel of communications below Mt. Fuji. It has been illustrated and described in detail by practically every important architectural magazine in the world. Its image is known to every architectural student and keeps appearing in variations on a good many of their drawing boards. It looks like a visionary drawing of the Metabolism Group materialized. It is another milestone in the career of Kenzo Tange.

Tange, born in 1913, is now widely recognized as one of the greatest living architects. He has received high honors in many countries, including the Gold Medal of the Royal Institute of British Architects in 1965 and the Gold Medal of the American Institute of Architects in 1966; he has an international practice which includes projects in the United States and the Middle East, as well as the city plan for Skopje, Yugoslavia—a commission won in an invited competition conducted by the United Nations.

He came quickly but surely to the international scene. His creative career, which began with the Hiroshima Peace Hall, 1949–56, follows a search for what he has called the "essential and progressive function" of each building, the typifying or symbolic form of the activity being sheltered.[11] Two formal themes interweave through his works. One may be called the "trabeation theme," for it is based on simple post-and-beam construction—a significant element of the tradition—gradually blown up by Tange to colossal scale. In his early Kagawa Government Office, 1955–58, he translated from the traditional timber to concrete the device of the overshooting beam. In the Kurashiki City Hall of 1958–60, the beams expanded until the gray mass of their concrete dominated all other elements, and windows disappeared behind the slits between beams. In the Plan for Tokyo (1960), whole buildings became beams supported high above the ground, or the water, on vertical service towers.

He started work on his first real project on this theme in 1961—

an office headquarters for the Dentsu Advertising Company, its twenty stories conceived as a giant lattice-beam spanning high above the street between the only two supports, which were a pair of elevator and service shafts set more than 30 meters apart (*Fig. 103*). The building site was in the Tsukiji area of Tokyo, lying beside the Ginza district and Tokyo Expressway No. 1. Tange replanned the whole area, extending the Dentsu lattice-beam structure to a three-dimensional network of beam-buildings which he proposed to levitate crisscross, on service masts, leaving a continuous open cityscape below (*Fig. 104*). Hideo Yoshida, the president of the Dentsu Company, keenly encouraged the Tange team. His building was to be the first, spurring on the redevelopment of the whole district. Just at this time a revision in the building code permitted the skyscrapers which now begin to dot Tokyo, and Tange planned some of his beam-offices nearly 130 meters high. Then his patron, Yoshida, died. The plan has gone no further, although the Dentsu building proceeded in much modified form. However, in the meantime, the Yamanashi project came to Tange and it gave him the opportunity to build for the first time the three-dimensional space network and to develop the trabeation principle to the scale when posts and beams became the actual working and living spaces of the building (*Fig. 114*).

Concurrently, Tange developed a second theme of plastic form. He seized every opportunity for this, which meant in effect whenever one large unsubdivided space was the main requirement of the building. This phase of his work built up through various hyperbolic and advanced geometrical forms to a climax in his buildings for the Tokyo Olympic Games in 1964. His commission for the Games was the National Gymnasium, which in fact consisted of a great covered pools building with seats for 15,000 spectators and a smaller multipurpose sports pavilion seating 4,000, as well as dining places, offices, and so on.

Tange put the accessory spaces in a low rectilinear podium whose roof was a promenade broken by snorkels to subterranean spaces and supported by massive buttresses. Then he planned the two gymnasiums near either end of this great podium, and decided to construct them in light tensile steel (*Fig. 105*).

Tension had been exploited imaginatively before this by several creative architects—notably Frei Otto and Eero Saarinen—and Tange has used it elsewhere for purely practical reasons; in 1967 he put a suspended roof on the Tosho printing plant at Hara-machi to provide a huge uninterrupted floor space. But it is fairly safe to say that no one before or since the 1964 Olympics has built a tensile structure with such confidence and conviction and sensitivity to the sculptural and monumental potentialities of the principle.

The big pools building has a roof hung in two separate sections from either side of a central catenary skylight which is slung between two great masts. Steel ties run out either side to be attached to the backs of the humped seating galleries. These steel ties pull the sides of the skylight apart, opening up a slit eye or cigar shape to the sky (*Fig. 106*).

The smaller pavilion is like a more frivolous sister of the pools building. It has a circular plan with a single eccentric towering mast from which radial cables are hung (*Fig. 107*). The bigger pools building is a majestic, almost symmetrical space, soaring blandly up the masts at each end, almost wholly revealed at first glance. The smaller building offers subtler delights. To enter it is a unique experience. It is a giant snail shell made mostly of wood and a gray-brown paint on steel. Overhead the space is gathered in by the roof as in an inverted counterclockwise whirlpool and is finally sucked up the dark, narrow, upended well beside the mast.

Both forms were developed after long work by Tange and his team on large scale models, shaping and adjusting, not merely for engineering efficiency but also for purely visual composition. To this extent they are sculptural. However, the intense interwoven logic of the visible form and the structure and the function soon become apparent on investigation, dispelling a first impression of arbitrary beauty, and tying the buildings to the classic mainstream of architecture.

In St. Mary's Tokyo Cathedral (1965), Tange again used a structural shape, this time the twisted plane, in concrete, as the basis of a plastic or sculptural form which he first devised mathematically then refined visually after long work on a model (*Fig. 108*). The essence of the cathedral's form is a kite-shaped ground plan from which rise mighty slab walls which are twisted so that, by the time they reach the top more than 30 meters overhead, they have folded in and formed between them a skylight cross in the proportions of the conventional crucifix. It is glazed; a window on to Heaven, you might say (*Fig. 109–110*).

Some of the more recent work produced from the office of Kenzo Tange and his team is less majestic. A certain contrived quality creeps in at times, especially in the smaller work, leading some Japanese critics to speculate about a change in the Tange style. But one must remember that it is a team, a large and busy one, and Kenzo Tange, a modest and kind man, does not want to dominate every design even if he had the time to do it. In the bigger projects where Tange himself is clearly in control, such as the theme center for Osaka's Expo 70, the personal Tange touch, of an idea which seems at once so brilliantly new yet so solidly established, is as sure and undeviating as ever.

Most of Tange's architectural inventions have started chain reactions, first through Japan and in many cases around the world, often losing most of their point on the way. The Tange vision has traveled best in the epoch-making building which has already been mentioned —the Yamanashi Press and Radio Center.

The variety of functions that had to be accommodated in this complex—office space, shops, printing works, broadcasting studios, distribution points, all with their different demands—gave Tange a perfect opportunity to develop, at the small scale of a single building, his ideas which could accommodate a city. First, he set up a grid of vertical service shafts (*Fig. 114*). He happened to make these cylindrical, largely no doubt to symbolize their basic duty as columns, and he stuck corbel blocks on the cylinders' sides, offering a grip to other elements of the construction. Inside the shafts he put the air conditioning, the stairs (*Fig. 113*) and the various grades of elevators needed for people and paper. He then planned the floors of offices, plant, and studios as beams spanning between the shafts, and arranged them in the places best suited to their functions (*Fig. 112*).

The drama of the building, the secret of its international influence, lies in the fact that not all the spaces between the vertical shafts or cores were required. Unoccupied voids remained here and

103. *The Dentsu Advertising Company building model of 1961; under construction 1968, Tokyo.*

104. *The Tsukiji Area project, model, Tokyo, 1960.*

there. These voids are rationalized by the architect and by admiring critics as spaces for expansion, also temporarily pleasant for use as roof gardens. There were more such voids in Tange's original scheme but pressure of economy while planning reduced, to Tange's regret, the number and the size of the voids. It is true that they allow space for expansion, and unused corbels on the sides of the shafts, inviting future additions, dramatize this fact. But it is also undeniable that the building would never have caught the world's imagination if the budget had been tightened even more and all the voids had needed to be filled from the start. As it is, there are just enough voids to demonstrate the fact that the building is capable of change and growth without interference to its formal unity, and to demonstrate externally, at a glance, the three-dimensional communications grid which is the basis of Tange's urban design philosophy.

The Yamanashi Center, although it is the only concrete manifestation so far of all the visions of Tange and the Metabolists for a remade world, is not a very big building. It was, Tange admits, at about the critical point of size to demonstrate his theories. But the

105. *National Gymnasium for the Olympic Games, Tokyo, 1964.*

106. *National Gymnasium for the Olympic Games, pools building, interior.*

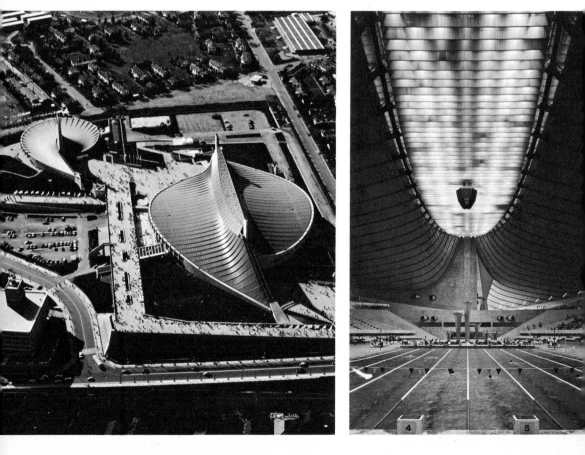

fact is that it was, happily, just big enough, and the voids were just wide enough to make the image and its message carry around the world. Suddenly the service shafts of projects on drawing boards everywhere seemed to change from Louis Kahnian rectilinear pylons to Tangean cylinders.

In 1967, in the Ginza district of Tokyo, Tange built another newspaper office block in a variation on the same theme (*Fig. 111*). This time, however, the conditions were very different. The scale was well below the critical point of size. The site was a tiny triangular corner lot. Tange had room for only one cylindrical service shaft. He sent this towering 63 meters into the air, cantilevering small lumps of office floors off either side. The principle on which he has been working for so long was here elevated to its zenith while simultaneously being reduced, in terms of practical economy, to absurdity. That is Japan.

For all the success that Tange has already earned, his talent always seems to be on the point of bursting out beyond his opportunities, as if he, like his country, can't wait for tomorrow.

107. *National Gymnasium for the Olympic Games. Left, smaller pavilion; right, pools building.*

108. *St. Mary's Cathedral, Tokyo, 1965.*

109. *St. Mary's Cathedral, interior.*

110. *St. Mary's Cathedral, skylight.*

111. *The Shizuoka building, Ginza, Tokyo, 1967.*

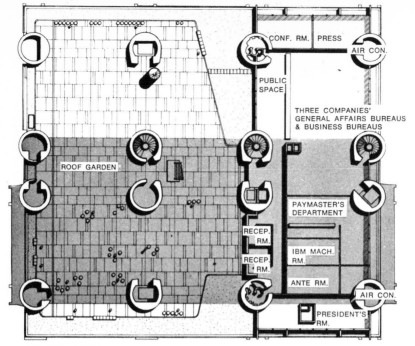

FOURTH-FLOOR

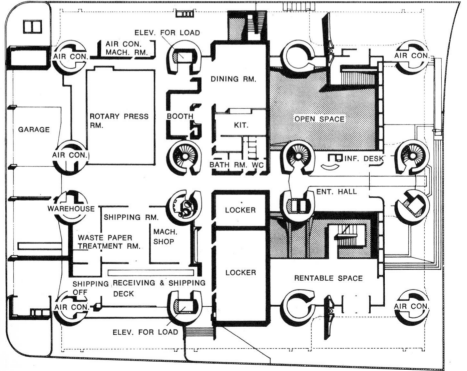

FIRST-FLOOR *scale: 1/500*

112. *The Yamanashi Press and Radio Center, first and fourth floor plans.*

113. *The Yamanashi Press and Radio Center, stairwell.*

114. *The Yamanashi Press and Radio Center, Kofu, 1967.*

NOTES

1. Kazuo Shinohara, "A Theory of Residential Architecture," *The Japan Architect (International Edition of Shinkenchiku)*, October 1967, 39.
2. *The Japan Architect*, December 1967, 21.
3. Kunio Mayekawa, Preface to *Contemporary Architecture of the World* (Shokokusha Publishing Co., Tokyo, 1961).
4. *The Japan Architect*, September 1966, 76.
5. *The Japan Architect*, September 1966, 48.
6. *World Architecture 2* (Studio Vista, London, 1965), 13.
7. *The Japan Architect*, December 1967, 78.
8. Noriaki Kurokawa, "Two Systems of Metabolism," *The Japan Architect*, December 1967, 80.
9. Hiroshi Hara, "Abundant Creativity," *The Japan Architect*, December 1966, 33.
10. Kazuo Shinohara, "A Theory of Residential Architecture," *The Japan Architect*, October 1967, 39.
11. See Robin Boyd, *Kenzo Tange* (George Braziller, Inc., New York, 1962).

PRINCIPAL JAPANESE JOURNALS
OF ARCHITECTURE

THE JAPAN ARCHITECT

International Edition of Shinkenchiku
Shinkenchiku-Sha Co., Ltd.
No. 31-2, 2-Chome Yushima
Bunkyo-Ku, Tokyo-To

The only English-language architectural magazine, giving a broad, unbiased view of Japanese building. Little or no editorial comment. Many illustrations, and articles by Japanese critics and architects well translated from the original journal, *Shinkenchiku.*

JAPANESE LANGUAGE
SPACE DESIGN (S D)

Kajima Institute Publishing Co., Ltd.
5-13, Akasaka 6-Chome
Minato-Ku, Tokyo-To

A monthly journal of art and architecture. Only the name is in English. Determinedly avant-garde, adventurous in format, with wide-ranging coverage of architecture, design, pop art, mass media, etc.

TOSHI JUTAKU (Urban Housing)

A monthly journal of Japanese and foreign architecture. By the same publishers as *Space Design*, but more sober and with the focus on urban housing in Japan and overseas.

KENCHIKU BUNKA (no English equivalent)

The Shokokusha Publishing Co., Ltd.
25 Sakamachi, Shinjuku-Ku, Tokyo-To

Straightforward illustrated reporting of recent buildings.

KENCHIKU NENKAN (Annual of Architecture in Japan)

Mr. Yoshihisa Miyauchi
Institute of Architectural Journalism
Dai 2 Aoi Mansion No. 302
6-1-8 Roppongi
Mijato-Ku, Tokyo-To

An authentic, impartial survey.

THE KENTIKU

Chugai-Shuppan-Sha
Fukuroku Biru (Building)
Tsukasa-Cho
Kanoa
Chiyoda-ku, Tokyo-To

An unadventurous, well-illustrated record of Japanese and some foreign architecture.

INDEX

SOURCES OF ILLUSTRATIONS

All photographs are reproduced with the permission of the architects.

1. *Japan Architect*, Tokyo.
2. From the office of Kiyonori Kikutake, Tokyo.
3. From the office of Noriaki Kurokawa, Tokyo.
4–7. *Shinkenchiku*, Tokyo.
8. *Japan Architect*, Tokyo.
9. © Takashi Oyama, Tokyo.
10. From the office of Jun'ichiro Ishikawa, Tokyo.
11. Shigeo Okamoto; copyright, Shokokusha, Tokyo.
12. Shiro Seki, Tokyo.
13. Osamu Murai, Tokyo; copyright, Shokokusha, Tokyo.
14–15. Masao Arai, Tokyo; © Shinkenchiku-Sha Co., Ltd., Tokyo.
16–17. © Y. Futagawa, Tokyo.
18. © Y. Ishimoto, Kanagawa-Ken.
19. © Y. Futagawa, Tokyo.
20. From the office of Kiyonori Kikutake, Tokyo.
21. © Takashi Oyama, Tokyo.
22. Taisuke Ogawa; © Shinkenchiku-Sha Co., Ltd., Tokyo.
23. © Osamu Murai, Tokyo.
24. From the office of Kiyonori Kikutake, Tokyo.
25–28. Shigeo Okamoto; copyright, Shokokusha, Tokyo.
29. *Japan Architect*, Tokyo.
30–32. Shigeo Okamoto; copyright, Shokokusha, Tokyo.
33. From the office of Masato Otaka, Tokyo.
34. Taisuke Ogawa; © Shinkenchiku-Sha Co., Ltd., Tokyo.
35. Osamu Murai, Tokyo; copyright, Shokokusha, Tokyo.
36. Taisuke Ogawa; © Shinkenchiku-Sha Co., Ltd., Tokyo.
37–38. From the office of Fumihiko Maki.
39. Masao Arai, Tokyo; © Shinkenchiku-Sha Co., Ltd., Tokyo.
40–42. Shigeo Okamoto; copyright, Shokokusha, Tokyo.
43. Yasuhiro Ishimoto, Kanagawa-Ken.
44. Osamu Murai, Tokyo.
45. Shiro Seki, Tokyo.
46. © Y. Futagawa, Tokyo.
47. Kouji Kawaguchi, Yamaguchi.
48. Osamu Murai, Tokyo.
49. Masao Arai, Tokyo.
50. Osamu Murai, Tokyo.
51–53. Y. Futagawa, Tokyo.
54–56. Y. Futagawa, Tokyo.
57. Takashi Oyama, Tokyo.
58. Osamu Murai, Tokyo.
59. Takashi Oyama, Tokyo.
60. *Japan Architect*, Tokyo.
61–62. Akio Kawasumi, Tokyo.
63. Osamu Murai, Tokyo.
64. From the office of Kazuo Shinohara, Tokyo.

65. Osamu Murai, Tokyo.

66. From the office of Kazuo Shinohara, Tokyo.

67–69. From the office of Yoshinobu Ashihara, Tokyo.

70. Y. Futagawa, Tokyo.

71. Masao Arai, Tokyo.

72.–73. From the office of Yoshinobu Ashihara, Tokyo.

74–75. Y. Futagawa, Tokyo.

76. Masao Arai, Tokyo; © Shinkenchiku-Sha Co., Ltd., Tokyo.

77. Masao Arai, Tokyo.

78. Osamu Murai, Tokyo.

79. Shigeo Okamoto.

80. Masao Arai, Tokyo; © Shinkenchiku-Sha Co., Ltd., Tokyo.

81–82 Masao Arai, Tokyo; © Shinkenchiku-Sha Co., Ltd., Tokyo.

83. Y. Futagawa, Tokyo.

84. From *Encyclopédie de l'Architecture, Constructions Modernes*, vol. XI, pl. 5, 1937 (Editions Albert Morance, Paris).

85–86. Toshio Tahira, Osaka.

87–88. Y. Futagawa, Tokyo.

89. From the office of Junzo Sakakura, Tokyo.

90. *Japan Architect*, Tokyo.

91. M. Outsuka, Tokyo.

92. Y. Takase, Tokyo.

93–94. Yoshio Watanabe.

95. T. Ohashi, Tokyo; Shokokusha, Tokyo.

96. Yoshio Watanabe.

97–99. From the office of Murano and Mori, Osaka.

100. Akio Kawasumi, Tokyo.

101–102. From the office of Murano and Mori, Osaka.

103–104. *Japan Architect*, Tokyo.

105. From the office of Kenzo Tange, Tokyo.

106. Y. Futagawa, Tokyo.

107. Osamu Murai, Tokyo.

108. Shigeo Okamoto.

109–110. Masao Arai, Tokyo; © Shinkenchiku-Sha Co., Ltd., Tokyo.

111. Osamu Murai, Tokyo.

112. *Japan Architect*, Tokyo.

113–114. Shigeo Okamoto.

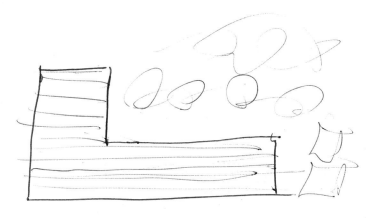